THE CANCER MONOLOGUE PROJECT

Edited by

Tanya Taylor and Pamela Thompson

MacAdam/Cage Publishing
155 Sansome Street, Suite 550
San Francisco, CA 94104
www.macadamcage.com
Copyright © 2002
ALL RIGHTS RESERVED.

Library of Congress Cataloging-in-Publication Data

The cancer monologue project / compiled by Tanya Taylor & Pamela Thompson.
    p. ; cm.
    ISBN 1-931561-22-2(hardcover : alk. paper)
    1. Cancer–Patients–Biography. 2. Cancer–Psychological aspects.
    [DNLM: 1. Neoplasms–psychology–Personal Narratives. 2. Neoplasms–
    psychology–Popular Works. 3. Survivors–Personal Narratives.
    4. Survivors–Popular Works. QZ 201 C2147 2002]
    I. Taylor, Tanya, 1964– II. Thompson, Pamela, 1959–

    RC265.5 .C36 2002
    362.1'96994'00922–dc21

                                                                2002009687

Manufactured in the United States of America.
10 9 8 7 6 5 4 3 2 1

Photography by Dorie Hagler.
Book and jacket design by Dorothy Carico Smith.

THE CANCER MONOLOGUE PROJECT

Edited by

Tanya Taylor and Pamela Thompson

MacAdam/Cage

ABOUT THE CANCER MONOLOGUE PROJECT

Tanya Taylor and Pamela Thompson

The Life Monologue Project is an organization that offers free writing and performance workshops to people living with cancer, HIV and AIDS. What you're about to read are monologues from three workshops that were held in Santa Fe, New Mexico. These monologues were created in two-weekend workshops with ten participants whose lives have been affected by cancer—either their own or that of a loved one. We have developed a process that supports people, most of whom have no prior experience with creative writing or performing, in crafting monologues—in this case, about living with cancer.

The workshops culminate in a public performance of the pieces in which the workshop participants share their stories. The effect of these performances on the participants and the audience members is profound. For participants recovering from cancer, these workshops offer an opportunity to reflect upon and make sense of their experience with cancer. For participants with poor prognoses, these workshops offer a chance to express what they most need to say, and to perhaps find closure. For the audience members it is a deeply intimate invitation to create a bridge of compassion, understanding and support for these people and their experiences.

We would like to invite you, the reader, to take a front-row seat as these thirty brave people share their stories of courage, heart and hope.

Contents

FOREWORD

Joanna Bull

There is no single way to describe the moment when cancer walks in the door and takes a front-row seat in the theater of your life. But not uncommonly, people will speak of a sizzling, searing, numbing sense of disbelief and a throbbing question: *Is this real?*

As founder of Gilda's Club Worldwide, an international network of free cancer support communities where men, women, children and their families and friends gather together to give and receive social and emotional support, I have encountered that question countless times, and as many times have seen people find their own personal answers. The dreamlike quality of the moment of diagnosis is in its own good time replaced by a sense of reality crafted with urgency or avoidance, grace or despair, depending on how the pieces of one's personal story are sorted out.

When reality is fashioned in the company of others who are going through the same thing, it is bound to have more truth and purposefulness. At Gilda's Club, "members" of the elite club that Gilda Radner said she would rather not belong to gather at their own clubhouse to share support and networking groups, lectures, workshops and social events for anyone touched by cancer. *The Cancer Monologue Project* is quintessential Gilda's Club workshop material, and we're so proud that Tanya Taylor and Pamela Thompson and each of the monologue writers have chosen to share with us the many benefits of their creation.

The stories in this volume are rich with questions asked by their authors, all of whom are living with cancer. Along the way, we learn that there are few answers, right or wrong, and none that are definitive. But in order to *live with cancer, whatever the outcome,* these storytellers have found a way to respond to that primordial first question, refusing to play out a scenario in which they are merely acted upon. In these stories, art and reality combine to strip each other of illusion and deliver immediate and authentic human truths, told by women and men who report directly from the expertise that comes from their experience.

The Cancer Monologue Project takes off from that first chaotic moment of disequilibrium and lays bare the flood of sensation and experience that follows, in story after story of hard-honed revelation, nakedness and humor. Each is distinctly individual and personal, no two the same. Commonality lies in the questions and in the inventiveness of each human response. *This is my story, this is where I end up when I tell it, exactly here, right now, and yes, it is real.*

The social and emotional issues that emerge with cancer are all to be found here, in rampant display: The agony of waiting for test results; looking very hard for humor as hair and eyelashes bite the dust; searching for meaning in the dissolution of life as one knows it; relationship shifts that are momentous; considering alternative treatments; hope, fear, joy, trust, good news, bad news, self-love, self-hate, vulnerability, loss, food, sex, secrets, choices, anger, depression, anxiety, pain, relief, control; and how to redefine control in the new world of living with cancer.

At a time when life in all its vitality and splendor has become more precious than ever, it is wonderfully paradoxical that looking in the mirror of death is what lends life its luminosity. The questions asked by these storytellers may not all be answered, but each of them leads directly to personal revelation that is of immense meaning to all of us, whether ill or well. The storytellers' questions are our own. We ask them for ourselves, as we read along. Here are just a few of those questions, and glimpses of our storytellers' responses.

"What does the amazing gift of time mean, and how can I utilize it most fully?" asks Nancy Henry, whose loneliness has shaped much of her life. *"Will there be enough time for me, for all of us, to be who we want to be? Will we be caught short?"* Nancy's story poses question after question that shows the lessons she has learned about loss of innocence, forgiveness, love and yearning for tranquility.

Michael Burt asks, following an epiphany that leads to a new definition of grace, *"What touched me when I was so sick? What reached me in a way no prayer ever has?"* Michael has peered through the retch of vomiting to behold the behind of an attending nurse, "an ass as shapely and perfect as a nectarine made personally by God Herself." His honesty and passion don't stop there.

"What does it mean to be a cancer 'survivor,' when you've already lived through the Holocaust and already said goodbye a thousand times? I know that it is all right for me to say goodbye to the strong person who was me, and admit that I no longer have that strength," answers Lisa Avedon.

"Good grief, now what?" asks Ron Christman. A software engineer turned sometime poet, Ron revels in the pure love he feels for his wife of many years, fears dependency, allows himself to care and, at last, to think with both sides of his brain. How far he has come from the small, dusty town in South Dakota, where work was scrabble-hard and rare tears shared with his father made a defining moment.

"How do I pray when I'm too sick to try?" asks Lena Albert. Become mythic, create ritual, breathe the sacred breath and "fly free in the spaciousness that is God's love," she answers for us. On her way to that truth, Lena gives us perspective on the abandonment, fear and self-hatred that so often accompany cancer. "There is nothing con-

stant but change," she tells us between nibbles of humor and irony.

"How do you know when it is time to leave?" is the question asked by Deborah Gunderman, whose story is a dramatic narrative of that very change; of deep friendship, small victories and goals achieved, of a gigantic uprooting leading "to the hope of renewal, healing and life." How does it feel? "Leaving is *so* bittersweet," Deborah reflects, showing us the ambiguity that follows us wherever we go.

"How could the people who designed this hospital be so insensitive?" asks Dr. Janet Greene, who gives us the perspective of a physician treated by physicians, and allows us to recognize that the feeling of safety many of us derive from "believing that doctors would always be there" leads to a false sense of security. Today, she is "a very different kind of doctor" who can support her patients' decisions about their own lives, one who realizes "how completely personal and extraordinary each person's journey is."

"Can a Woman With One Breast and No Hair Be Sexy?" is the title question asked by Judi Jaquez, whose description of mastectomy and chemotherapy is laced with yet more irony and humor. Judi poses an additional question pertaining to chemicals and the acclaimed power of the blood/brain barrier: "Then what takes over your brain, making familiar words disappear, eliminating decision-making powers, letting one observe things without recording a memory of it?"

"Do I only have five years left? How could that be? I'm supposed to live until my eighties and nineties like my grandparents," says Judy Kiphart, who questions yet another false sense of security that most of us nurture and protect. In reporting that cancer has shaken her faith, Judy renews the question that all of us can ask over and over again: *"What is faith and what does it mean to me?"*

"Today I sit with a group of other people who have all been

touched by cancer in some manner, either directly as a survivor or as a mother, brother, wife of someone whom they cherished. We are sharing our stories through writing," obverves Alice Kitselman, in "Waiting to Get a Life." The process that leads to these collected stories, brilliantly devised and refined by theater artists Tanya Taylor and Pamela Thompson, is born from the creation of a community of storytellers. The results are here, vibrant and alive. As with all stories, we can fill in the voices and faces ourselves. They are our own.

And as with all stories that have taken shape around illness, or any human experience, we see two possibilities before us. One option is to remain frozen in the story, to tell and re-tell it, to revert to the story as one's sole reality, to live and re-live the story and believe that it is final, irreversible, the only truth. Questions are no longer asked.

Our other option is to work inward as these storytellers have done, to the essence of one's individual truth; to tell it, and let it go, to make room for new truths. These stories are surely offered up to all of us who are ill and seek to learn how to live with illness. They are there for those of us who seek meaning and purpose in everyday experience. Their merit is also shared with us. Their inspiration is a gift. Their truth challenges us to seek our own truth, and to tell it as thoughtfully and as honestly.

CANCER AND OTHER TRAVELS

Deborah Milton Spaulding

When the surgeon introduced himself and told me I had ovarian cancer, I was surprised, but not particularly frightened. I was so sick, I was already pretty sure I was dying. The doctor was telling me he had a plan; he could fix me up and send me home. My operation would be in six days. I was pleased to know he thought I'd live that long.

I didn't cry. My husband, Tony, didn't cry and neither did my two sisters, who waited outside my hospital room for the reading of the verdict. Nobody cried. We just talked about what was next and anything any of us knew about cancer, which wasn't very much; none of our family or any of our close friends had gotten it.

The only cancer story I could think of was Brian Piccolo, played by James Caan on TV. I remembered a horrid scene where the great American athlete is in a bathtub screaming in pain. I wasn't in a screaming kind of pain...yet.

My first symptom of the disease appeared in the Highlands of New Guinea at the annual Sing Sing. Hundreds of dancers on an open field, dressed in outrageous tribal regalia. It was hot and humid and I was fighting a cold, but having the absolute time of my life, running around the field shooting photos.

After six or eight rolls of film, I left the field and watched from a shaded area. When the performance ended and I got up to leave, I felt a horrendous pain in my thighs. When I tried to walk, my legs didn't want to move; it was like I had lead in my shoes. Every step was slow and deliberate and excruciating.

When I met up with Tony at the van, I didn't say anything about my crippled legs. I'd deduced they were a symptom of dropping out of yoga class and turning fifty. Apparently, I no longer had the muscle tone to squat for seven hours taking photographs. But only I had to know that. And the next day they were fine.

We spent another week in New Guinea, then flew to the Philippines to do some buying for our antique business. It was nighttime and raining when we got to our hotel, but having never been there before, I couldn't wait to go out and experience life on the streets of Manila.

We strolled out of the hotel under a yellow umbrella the doorman lent us, but only made it a block or two when my legs began to punk out again. They didn't really hurt this time; it was more like I'd lost some motor skills. I couldn't keep up with Tony, and couldn't explain why. The next day it was the same thing.

Then my belly began to swell. I had no appetite and wasn't eating, but every day, for no reason at all, it got bigger and more uncomfortable. Something was very wrong, and when the Philippine doctor couldn't help me, I knew it was time to go home. The first flight we could get back to the States was two days later. While waiting, my belly continued to swell and I grew sicker and weaker. Every time I closed my eyes, I saw images of Jesus, which didn't exactly comfort me.

By the time we crossed the Pacific and entered the emergency room in L.A., I looked like a worn-out middle-aged woman about to deliver a pony. After a battery of tests, I was admitted to a room, and the next day I met the surgeon. I'd already had plenty of time to contemplate the worst; I'd even rehearsed a couple of farewell speeches on the plane.

I wasn't afraid of dying. At fifty, I was pretty satisfied with my life.

I'd had more privileges, opportunities and comfort than most of the human race. I had made my contributions to society, and had no unfinished business I could think of. My daughter was grown and out on her own, and I had no future plans that might change the course of history. If this was it for me, it was a great ride, a little hair-ball at the end, but all in all I'd gotten a pretty good seat in this life.

After surgery, and before starting chemo, I spent an afternoon work-ing on creative visualization with a Tao healer. She was amazing. Before we got started, I told her that I had reconciled with God and death and that I was okay with it. I was sincere and thought she'd appreciate how spiritually together and stoic I was. But no, she pursed her lips and in her rich German accent said, "I zinks you might do a little better if you zink more about why you vant to live."

I also met with an acupuncturist, who, as luck would have it, was also a licensed therapist. She, too, thought I might stand a fighting chance if I'd embrace life a little more and death a little less.

It was beginning to register: if I was going to leave this world with any respect at all, I had to abandon my peace with death and deter-mine I was going to live. That's when it got hard. When you don't want something so badly, it's less painful when you don't get it. I never tried out for cheerleader in high school. I knew my odds of making it, and was smart enough to know I'd be investing a lot of time and effort just to get my heart broken. Instead, I tried out for drill team, where I thought my chances were pretty good, but I still didn't make the team. And my heart did break.

Now, with a twenty percent chance of winning, I was committed to a contest I never signed up for. The first step was to let go of the hand of the angel of death and forget I ever saw her sorry face. I did a pretty good job of it, too, especially with the progress I was making with chemotherapy. The more wretched I felt after treatment, the more I knew the poison was working; if it could make a big girl like me puke and gag, imagine what it was doing to those pissant little cancer cells. My finest hours of optimism were spent with my head in the toilet.

The angel of death continued to hover, we just weren't friends anymore. Now that we were on different teams, I demoted her to the angel of doubt, and for the sake of my loved ones kept her a secret.

I was three months into treatment when she got me at the Wal-Mart store. I broke down while pondering the purchase of a Christmas tree skirt. I'd never actually owned one. I always thought that, for less money, I could make a nicer one myself, but never did. The one I held in my hand was just lovely, as nice as any I could make, and cheap—I was at Wal-Mart. I could tell it wanted to go home with me. But, thinking this could very well be my last Christmas, I put it down. I knew Tony wouldn't put up a tree when I'm gone.

To him, decorating a tree is a whole lot of work for something that's not all that attractive when you're done. It's me who loves the tacky tinsel and glitter. I love everything about Christmas: the mailbox stuffed with greetings; the homemade cookies, hand-dipped candles, summer harvest in a jar; the making time for friends, a marathon of feasts; the same old carols everyone knows by heart. I even like fruitcake. Not Tony. In general, the whole aesthetic of Christmas is a little too contrived and sweet for him. It's hard for a man who's spent his entire adult life studying the art and ritual of tribal cultures to feel inspired by a calico angel or reindeer made of clothespins. That's because he didn't make them and wasn't around in the seventies when I was "a little bit country." Too bad that was the decade I had the most time on my hands.

So how could I justify paying $24.99 for a Christmas tree skirt knowing it would soon be just another useless thing for him to trip over, a new addition to the tomb of the broken VCRs and dead computer monitors, buried beneath ancient tax records, future building materials, abandoned art projects, and various other bad ideas residing in our garage? If it was to end up on anyone's water supply, I knew it wouldn't be any time soon.

I picked it up again to examine it more closely. Made in China. The matter settled, I put it down and suddenly burst into tears. Oblivious to the crowd of passing shoppers, I stood in the middle of Wal-Mart and cried like a two-year-old. They weren't tears over China and they weren't "poor me" tears, either. Tenuous as it may be, my life wasn't so terrible. I was mourning the loss of Christmas.

I told Behty, my acupuncturist/therapist, about the incident. I was sorry I had to admit to these feelings, but I could tell her things I couldn't tell my family. On occasion, I got her to cry with me, but never once did she say, "Don't talk like that."

My girlfriend Jano and her husband drove out from California to spend the holidays with us. Jano and I have been best friends for more than thirty years; she's more like a sister to me. We tell each other everything and keep no secrets. So when she commented on the Balinese sarong wrapped around the tree stand, I went ahead and told her about making a jackass out of myself at Wal-Mart. By the stricken look on her face, I knew immediately I'd made a mistake. She didn't want to hear any talk about this being my last Christmas.

What was I thinking? Maybe that she wouldn't have driven 900 miles over icy roads to spend our first Christmas together in ten years if she wasn't thinking this could be my last Christmas too. The cancer was new to all of us, and with it came new boundaries. Death and dying are not words to be used casually with your best friend in the whole world. I wanted to tell her I was sorry for talking foolishly, and that the angel of doubt really doesn't pester me very often, but instead let it go.

Christmas day we had a houseful of guests, and while I was busy attending to my duties as hostess, Jano was taking pictures. I didn't know she'd been desperately trying to get my attention until she strong-armed me and dragged me to the Christmas tree. "Now stand there so I can get a picture of your last Christmas." We both howled while I adjusted my turban and posed.

I'm out of treatment now, four months in remission. Everything is looking great, with the exception of my pitifully slow-growing hair. When I tell my sister how much I hate looking this way, she's surprised. "I thought you'd risen above that kind of thing by now."

Well, I had risen above it. I rose above a lot of things while walking with angels, and for that I'll be forever thankful for the experience of cancer. But with every familiar human feeling that returns, the more I know I'm back, and I'm going to fight like a mad dog to stay.

Christine Barber

I'm not a crier, but I cried that day. Wracking, can't-catch-your-breath sobs, as I sat in my car in the hospital parking lot. A woman glanced at me as she walked by, seeing my smeared mascara, blotchy lipstick and cheeks streaked with tears. She probably thought I was sad. The doctor had said the scan "looked good." I waited until I was alone in my car to break down in relief. I called everyone on my cell phone, telling them my scan was clean. The thyroid cancer that had spread to my lungs was gone. I cried more. I started my car and headed for the Glorieta Baptist Center. I wanted to walk in the prayer garden, the only green place I could think of in December. I needed to be outside, near God.

As I drove, I thought of the past year, the surgery, the radiation I had ten months ago. That damn radiation, where I sat for three days in a lead-lined room, my only constant visitor a hospital tech who checked me every few hours with some type of Geiger counter. Most of the room was covered in plastic, like when you visit your paranoid grandmother who Saran-wraps the sofa in case you spill something. The hospital put plastic on the phone, the toilet, the bed to protect them—from me, from my radioactivity. I was a radioactive danger to society. A prisoner in a lead-lined room who must be kept away from all the healthy people. The very nice doctors and very nice nurses who came in stood behind lead-lined screens, staring at me.

I drank bottle after bottle of Gatorade to coax the radiation out of my body, the sweet taste sticking to the roof of my mouth. I didn't think about the plastic, the Gatorade or the very nice nurses. I just made it all into an amusing story I told the people who called me on the plastic-covered phone. I described with a laugh the weird three-flush toilet ritual I had to perform and the visits from the Geiger-counter man. I didn't tell the callers about what the radiation was doing to me, seeping and creeping into my every cell. I didn't think about what it was doing to my ovaries, my eggs—my eggs that were now contaminated by radiation. I made jokes to my sister on the phone about how my unborn kids would be superheroes, the radiation giving them the ability to bend steel and talk to fish. I didn't tell her about my fears that I would now be childless.

I left the hospital after my three days and tried very hard not to think about that lead-lined room. I thought about work, school, guys, guacamole, anything but cancer. Did I really have cancer? Five months after I left the hospital, I was in Target, the bright, fluorescent lights giving everything a weird, radioactive glow. How the meaning of that word has changed for me. I don't even remember what I was shopping for, probably something innocuous like cotton balls, toothpaste or a lava lamp. Everyone at work had been telling me how "fabulous" I looked, but I always wondered if they were lying as they tried not to stare at the neon pink surgical scar across my neck. The other Target shoppers didn't even glance at my scar. I convinced myself that meant it wasn't noticeable, as I grabbed my cotton balls or lava lamp and headed to the checkout line. I plunked my purchases on the counter, not paying much attention to what I was doing, my mind, my eyes, my everything, on something else.

And then I heard, "Hey, it's the Scar Lady."

I looked up. I'd seen this cashier before. His face was pink with acne. He had piggy little eyes of a piggy little, nondescript color. He was tall and bony, not yet grown into his body.

For one tiny second that will stretch out for the rest of my life, I hated that stupid, idiotic sixteen-year-old boy. A boy who was only trying to be friendly in his awkward teenage way. I hated him because he made me remember that I'd had cancer. I hated him because he told the truth when no one else would. He saw my scar and, for once, unlike every single person before him, he didn't say I looked "fabulous." He saw my scar for what it was: horrible. He told it like it was. I mumbled "hello" to the boy and left as quickly as I could, not wanting him to see the anger in my eyes.

Five months later the doctor said my cancer was gone and that silly boy became nothing more than a funny story for me to tell at dinner parties.

That December day as I pulled into the prayer garden, I thought about making myself a bumper sticker that read "Make Way for the Scar Lady." I laughed at my own joke as I got out of the car, beaming, my face still wet with tears. I prayed and thanked God as I walked. I even got down on my knees in the icy mud. Hallelujah and all that. I found a quiet bench next to an unbelievably tall ponderosa pine and sat down to write in my journal. I wrote, "Today I walk in the garden of God," and thought "What a nice thing to put on a tombstone." My tombstone. Someday, fifty years from now. In the faraway future when I died of old age or an accident involving a llama and a Go-Kart, not cancer. I was joyous. I had always heard that word used in church songs and never understood it. That was my most joyous day. Isn't that pathetic? My most joyous day involved cancer. Not my graduation from college, not getting the big job. But a deadly illness.

How funny that day seems now. Not "ha, ha" funny, but horrible funny.

Almost a year after that day, I went to the doctor's office for a checkup. I sat on the examination table, my feet not reaching the ground, kicking my legs like some elementary school kid sent to the principal's office. I was there for a checkup. A simple checkup. Nothing more. Just a checkup like I had several times since finding out my cancer was gone.

The office was cold, but it always was. The nurse was looking at my chart, not at me. Always at my chart with all those bright green Post-it notes on the front that I couldn't read from a distance no matter how much I scrunched up my eyes. The nurse's brow was furrowed. Her red hair was wispy at the ends where it was dried from too much hair dye. I was bored. As always when I'm bored, I made a joke. I don't remember exactly what I said. Something about being in remission. I laughed, but she didn't. She seemed so hesitant, so unsure. She said something about "traces." She said the scan last year, the same scan the doctor said "looked good," showed traces of cancer. I still had cancer. I was confused, too confused to ask questions. Too confused to wonder why the doctor hadn't mentioned that I still had cancer during my last three office visits. Had it just never come up in conversation? The nurse said when the doctor told me the scan "looked good," he meant the cancer hadn't spread, not that it was gone.

I work in words. I know their power. The doctor had said it "looked good," the same as saying "You're cured," right? In journalism we call it paraphrasing a quote. I paraphrased that quote for a full year to my family, my friends, myself, telling everyone I was cured. The doctor said so when he saw my scan, didn't he? Or did I just hear what I wanted? Did I just want to forget so badly about lead-lined hospital rooms and awkward cashiers that I turned it around in my head?

I needed facts. I needed this nurse with her bad dye job to tell me facts. I hang on to facts like that pink security blanket I had as a kid, the one I clutched into pieces while warding off the monsters in my closet. But she told me nothing in her sidestepping medical-speak.

She just talked about "traces." I used to like that word. It sounds like it could be the name of an upscale apartment complex: "The Traces de Piñon—An exclusive apartment community in the beautiful Sangre de Cristo Mountains."

The nurse was nice and polite, bad hair and all; too polite to comment on how I melted into nothingness in front of her. I still think about that scene in the doctor's office like it was inside a snow globe, and I'm on the outside, shaking up the globe and peering inside at the falling snow. It's apart from me, not touching me. In some wonderland far away.

What now? What do I say to you now? I don't know the answer to that. I wish I had some nice, happy ending to give you, complete with a handsome prince and a Disney song. But the truth is I'm still furious and devastated. That about covers it. Not much more to say than that. Too furious and too devastated for words.

A Passenger

Lisa Avedon

I've been saying "goodbye" all of my life. I began saying goodbye in Germany, just before my third birthday, when my father died. He was the export manager for our family business and used his ability to travel on business to other European countries to deposit money in Holland, since it was becoming clear after the Nazis came into power that it would be difficult for Jews to remain in Germany. The Gestapo searched him when his train reentered Germany from Denmark and discovered a small notebook, the contents of which he could not explain to their satisfaction. They let him continue to Holland, but arrested my mother and held her at Gestapo headquarters in Munich, the city where we lived, to ensure his return. Knowing that he would be sent to a concentration camp if he returned and my mother would if he didn't, he committed suicide.

I always regretted not having been able to say goodbye to my father. My only memory of him was when he lifted me up to kiss me and I felt his scratchy face. And I didn't know the true story of his death until my son was three, when my mother finally was able to tell me the truth—it was easier for her to create and live with the fiction that he had died of a heart attack while on business in Amsterdam—and the rest of the family went along with her and was silent all those years.

I am sure that there are other things I don't remember from my short life in Nazi Germany. The reason I am sure is because of an experience I had in France about ten years ago. I was visiting a friend in Paris when we encountered a march protesting the expulsion of Sudanese refugees. I saw two gendarmes grab a man and throw him into an armored vehicle. I freaked out but didn't know why until I asked my brother, who is three and a half years older. He told me that I had seen the Gestapo do the same thing when I was four years old.

In May of that year, 1939, we said goodbye to Germany—my mother, grandmother, brother and I left on a ship that was supposed to land in Havana, Cuba. From there we were supposed to go to New Jersey to join my aunt, uncle and cousin. The ship, the *St. Louis,* was denied entry into Cuba. The captain tried to land in Miami. The U.S. government sent a Coast Guard ship to keep watch and make sure no one went ashore. Canada and every other country in North and South America denied us entry. We said goodbye to this hemisphere, sailed back to Europe, not knowing what was going to happen to us. My family and I were fortunate in saying goodbye to the St. Louis when we were put onto a freighter that took us to England. Two-thirds of the passengers were not as fortunate and were eventually exterminated by the Nazis in the death camps.

We lived in London for a while—my main memories of those months were fog and the smell of the gas masks we wore in the Underground, which became bomb shelters. We said goodbye to London when we were moved to Devon, where we lived in a boarding house next to a field where horses ran wild.

One day, I petted a colt, which then kicked me so hard that I had the bruise on my leg for a long time—I said goodbye to horses. We received our visas to the U.S., so I said goodbye to England.

Our ship arrived in New York harbor on December 23, 1939. We were greeted by Christmas decorations wherever we looked—something I had never seen—and by my uncle and aunt, my mother's twin who looked so much like my mother that it took me some time to tell them apart.

We lived together for four years, until my younger cousin was about to be born—then there wasn't enough room in the house, and I said goodbye again.

We moved into a tiny apartment in New York, where we lived for nine years until my mother remarried and moved to Milwaukee. I said goodbye to New York. I went to college in Milwaukee, graduate school first in Minneapolis, then New York, married, moved to Hastings-on-Hudson, New York, then to Canada—Waterloo, Ontario—divorced, moved to Toronto when I was asked by the Government of Ontario to initiate and administer a program for workers who lost their jobs in plant closures and downsizings, and finally here to Santa Fe. I've said goodbye to homes, places, people, and the colleges where I taught. Altogether, I've moved more than twenty times in my life—three-quarters of them in the first half of my life. I've said goodbye so often that one could think I would be used to it by now, but I'm not. The goodbye I think of most now is having to say goodbye to the two people I love the most—my daughter, Madeline, and my son, Roger.

Since my grandmother lived to be eighty-four, my mother, who was not very healthy, was eighty when she died, so I assumed that I would live at least as long as they did. I was healthy all my life—exercised, watched my diet, didn't smoke, drink—I was sure that it would be a very long time before I would have to say goodbye to my children, to everyone, to my life.

Being a cancer "survivor" is a phrase that keeps coming up—in my cancer support group, in the literature. There are many articles on the Web and many books with those words in the titles or subtitles. What does "survivor" mean? The dictionary defines surviving as "outliving, outlasting and continuing beyond the death of another or of an event." In regard to cancer, it just seems to mean that one is alive, because it can be a short time after diagnosis and treatment—when tests haven't found any more cancer cells—or a long time—I know people who were diagnosed with cancer twenty years ago and have been in remission ever since!

To me, having been diagnosed with Stage 4 breast cancer, being a cancer "survivor" is a wobbly thing—a loose term that just means I'm still alive but the beasts, the cancer cells, may have their way with me at any time. "Survivor" is a hard term for me to come to grips with at this point in my life, as I've been a Holocaust survivor since I was four.

So, in one sense, for me "survivor" means I am lucky to be alive and to have lived this much of my life as compared to those millions who were killed in the Holocaust. I had never before thought of the difference between dying from a disease and being murdered. Can I think of cancer as wanting to murder me as the Nazis did? Can I think of a disease that kills as a murderer? And, since I will be receiving treatment for the rest of my life, do I call myself a survivor?

In contrast was my experience last month when my children and I participated in a reunion of the passengers of the *St. Louis*, the ship that was turned back from Cuba. Our hosts, Progressive Vision International, a Christian organization, invited us to their All Americas Convocation, along with representatives from all of the countries in the hemisphere. Their invitation was a statement of repentance from the churches for not having protested when governments denied us refuge. The pin I'm wearing, a gift from our hosts, is an expression of their feelings about what happened. Most important, though, to me, is that during the reunion we were always referred to not as survivors but as "the passengers."

In another way I have been very lucky. Although my mother's life was so difficult, I realized when she became elderly that she had been depressed for a long time, but had always been very supportive of me, never had a negative word to say about anything I did.

What I learned from her was to try to do the same with my children, so I have always encouraged them and my reward is that they are successful in their careers, happy in their relationships, and since I was diagnosed, spend as much time as possible with me.

Last December I began a new course of treatment and my hair grew back—curly for the first time in my life. I'm losing weight because I have little appetite—soon I may be as thin as a model! People keep telling me how great I look. Well, I may look great, but I feel rotten. I don't want to hear that I look great when I don't feel great and have no idea if I will ever feel great again. So, I ask you, kind members of the audience, if you bump into me after the performance, and feel the words "you look great" are about to spill out of your mouths—please bite your tongues!

Finally, I've always prided myself on being strong and self-reliant. In my whole adult life, I feel that I've been able to deal quite effectively with the transitions I have made. And I have written and had published a number of articles on that subject. When I was preparing to end my marriage I worked everything out in regard to my children, our living arrangements and which of my friends, neighbors, and colleagues I could count on for support. I suppose that all the moves and changes I have had to make resulted in my being able to plan ahead—until now.

Recently, to my surprise, I've found myself with tears in my eyes when watching a film or a television program or reading. I've become aware that the experience of having a life-threatening illness—wondering whether the cancer or I will be in control—has transformed me, opened up another part of me. I now know that I don't always have to be—actually, do not have the energy to be—as strong as I once was. I know that it is all right for me to say goodbye to the strong person who was me and admit that I no longer have that strength. That I can accept help, and even ask for it from those who care about me. And that I have a choice as to how I label myself. I can think of myself as a passenger on another difficult life voyage that is taking me to places to which I have never before traveled.

Lisa now wants to add a third person to those she lists as loving the most: her grandson, Max Avedon Mirkin, born to her daughter on April 27, 2002.

Strawberries

Sylvia Vizcaya Alderson

To feel pure abandonment—that freedom, that joy—the feeling in my chest when I would walk to the bus and see blue sky, perfect blue sky, and song would rise from my soul. When I was a little girl, the rest of my family would go out for ice cream and I would push back the living room furniture and play "I Have Confidence" from *The Sound of Music*. Dancing, singing, free, wild, true—that was my abandonment. Then I grew up to be an adult, making sure that everything was in place. All the i's dotted and the t's crossed. Make sure that my handicapped sister had what she needed, make sure that my work was done right, see that everything was in place—there didn't seem to be time for that abandonment of my childhood—then wonderfully I found it again. Since I had been conditioned to appreciate work over leisure, my theater work was justified because I did work oh, so hard and there were those moments of complete, joyous abandonment, like before—often accompanied by music, with singing and dancing in a musical and the new sounds of accompaniment in gasps, tears, sniffles, sighs and laughter as I did comedies, farces, tragedies and dramas. I felt pure abandonment, immersed within my talent and skill, my heart and soul.

Then I found the cancer, of all times the opening weekend of a play. Slowly as I told people—family, colleagues, my boss, friends —of my diagnosis I saw the separation in their eyes and heard it in their voices.

For some it was the separation of caring, for others the burden of my illness, and for others fear. From all I felt abandonment. I couldn't breathe deeply for the fear clogging my lungs and diaphragm, I couldn't lift my eyes for the fear that would escape them, I couldn't hear from the tears that poured from others into my ears. How fair is it for people to tell me in small passing comments about people they've heard of who died from cancer. How fair is that? Is it just because I don't look like I am at death's door?

Okay, so hard but okay, tie on the scarf with a flair, paint or draw on the eyebrows. Try to pretend, from inside, that you can look at your reflection and say "not bad." Then lean on the counter and breathe. I've only been up for an hour but I'm tired, not fatigued, just feeling like every cell is sagging—weighted down with heavy beads. I look up at my reflection and grimace—time to get on with the day—must get to work. I've been told in small, indiscreet ways, directly and indirectly, I've missed a lot. I've been told, "I can't do your job, too." So sorry to have gotten cancer this summer—I really hadn't planned it. So sorry to have been out those first days after chemo, those few hours every day that first week of radiation. What about the ten-hour days I put in between chemos? I get angry inside but must breathe through that, too.

All those patrons coming up to the ticket counter to get their tickets—to see a show—too bad they can't hear me screaming inside. "You look so good," "How do you do it?" "You are so brave," "So amazing." *No, I'm not.* I feel like shit. I haven't a clue why my face isn't pink and green and purple and blue. Why my arms aren't dripping blood, why my scalp looks so innocent and white, not the deep hurting red I feel inside. So tired of hearing "You look so good." So tired of no one looking in my eyes for even one small moment and asking, "How do you feel?" then waiting, having the strength to listen to my answer. What, because I don't have the gray pallor, because I don't look like what you think someone with cancer should look like, I'm looking good? I've gained over twenty pounds, I have red scars on my face from chemo, I have new miles of cellulite to pad my passage through chemo-induced menopause.

It's horrible. Should I say thank you for not seeing that? But then you aren't seeing me.

My Jay, my wonderful husband, ran, pursued by demons of fear and apprehension and misunderstanding, bolted away to be productive—to teach, to work, to help others. He is such a good man. Shock of shocks, I was alone and didn't like it…needed an anchor, a hand, eyes, something to latch onto in those late-night, midday, early-morning hours of despair. No amount of telling myself how strong I am was going to bridge that chasm, this void of needing to breathe in safety and love.

I have always been so strong, always trusted me—that has been my mainstay. My soul has always been grounded in the strength of my body. I could walk forever, run, hike, lift, carry—I had strength, stamina and fortitude. Stamina and strength were my bylines. Now all that was gone and I was foundering. Most of my relationships were based on who I was as a strong, utilitarian person—they weren't based on me just being. I didn't let them be.

I was depleted to almost nothing, almost. I felt so little, so *less than*. I had never felt little even when I was five and reaching up to grasp my grandfather's hand or climbing up on my dog Lobo's back to ride him around the yard. Reading all the time gives you no sense of size, just the immensity of everything out there. I wondered why my mother didn't come here to be with me. I know she has to take care of my sister. Why can't I ever come first? I felt a small clutching in my heart.

Okay, so now it's time to turn this cancer, turn it back on itself and come out with new understanding, new stamina for self-realization. Hard to face the fact that I felt worthless without my physical strength, hard to realize now I need to be on the receiving end of help. Yet oh, so wonderful to watch, from inside, as my chosen family steps up and helps and becomes part of my renewed life. My doctors tell me that chemo attacks your body at the cellular level— how nice. I have been revamped, restructured. I am now hypo-glycemic thanks to the chemo. My poor body has hot flashes and bleeds as I ride the Hormone Hell roller coaster.

I may not like the physical me I see in the mirror, but I have begun to understand the insides of me a little better. The old resentments and hurt feelings that were dammed up behind my stamina have leaked into the sunshine and been washed away. I want to smile, just smile and sit. Not work, just sit and smile and be amazed that this is me doing only that and being happy. I have learned to get help for myself, to reach out to others about breast cancer in a way that is comfortable for me. My husband told me that women would look at my scarf-head then glance at my chest, fear lacing their eyes. I wanted to wheel in my tracks, smile and reach across the chasm of strangers and reassure. I want to displace fear with understanding and hope.

I remember being sixteen and feeling like a new person inside and out every two weeks. As I shed this skin of cancer treatment and move forward there is light, understanding. Strawberries that Susan and Irene left on my door when I got home from chemo; calls from my aunt (a survivor) and uncle from Chicago; the worried voices of my aunt and uncle who live here in Santa Fe; a calming talk from Mark, my friend surviving kidney disease; the sorbet Peg brought by; the chicken and rice Suzanne, a working, single mother of two, took the time to make (because she remembered I needed protein) and bring by; the kind bus driver who said "great hat"—all these seemingly small gifts that weren't small at all.

I've started to feel that wonderful abandonment again—in being able to walk my dogs, to ask for help, to reach out and take my hus-band's hand, to have soul-sight, to have the pure wondrous aban-donment in being able to live.

THE DEEPEST SURRENDER

Mary Tufft

I hadn't expected this to be so hard, this time of transition. This time of transition from preparing to die to living in limbo. I was told there was no visible cancer, then again at my appointment three months later, no visible cancer. I remember asking my oncologist on the day I got the news the second time, exactly what does this mean? She replied that it meant that they could not see cancer on the latest scan and that for now she would not recommend treatment. Her answer to my question so clear, so simply stated.

I left the cancer center in a daze. My wonderful and so knowledgeable, though much too busy, oncologist, Dr. Smith, and my incredibly supportive nurse Peggy, who for two years had so patiently sat to answer my multitude of questions. My list of well-researched questions about which combinations of chemotherapy drugs were currently having the best results. What was being recommended to minimize the side effects of these drugs? Questions about intraperitoneal photodynamic therapy and intravenous investigational murine monoclonal antibody studies. I could count on Dr. Smith and Peggy to answer all of my questions. That day I hadn't even pulled the list of questions from my purse because I had no visible cancer.

I walked out into the bright Albuquerque sun, stunned. I searched for those feelings of elation I would expect to have somewhere inside me. Instead I found that same question: "What exactly does this mean?" I had recurrent ovarian cancer, it was the killer, or one of them. Not the best cancer to have if one was going about the business of picking a cancer. The year before when the cancer recurred I had gone to M.D. Anderson Cancer Center for a second opinion. The doctor there was shocked that I was still working. I'm a teacher. I was told with sensitivity that this was a time to get clear on what I wanted to do with the time I had left.

The doctor told me there were no new treatments available to me now, but if "they" could keep me alive for two years, quite possibly some new, less toxic drug options would be available. These treatments could not be made available to me now. They were being used on mice and in fact, she shared excitedly, they had almost eradicated ovarian cancer in mice. I thought this was hilarious. I had the image of a tiny female mouse in a hospital gown, her belly shaved, the little mouse oncologist standing over her making a long vertical incision, performing a hysterectomy and continuing the snips here and there of more mouse tissue to send to the lab to determine if it were cancerous. Then I saw a chemo room. The room full of chairs, each with a reclining mouse, little arm outstretched, hooked up to an IV. The miniature chemo room filled to capacity with mice patients and a mouse family member or friend sitting by them gently stroking their forehead or holding the emesis pan, some providing a snack or quiet conversation. Although I could tell by the look on the doctor's face that she questioned the appropriateness of my laughter, I was thankful for the comic relief these images brought me during the intensity of my short visit to this well-respected cancer facility.

And now it was over a year since my appointment at M.D. Anderson and I had no visible cancer. I had gotten everything, or nearly everything, in order. Beneficiary for my slim public school retirement. Beneficiary for my even smaller IRA. Directive to physicians, power of attorney for healthy care.

I had even spent an afternoon carefully affixing masking-tape name labels on the bottom of furniture to make it easier for my things to be passed on. The antique oak bench which as a child I would set my coat on before climbing the stairs to the living area in my grand-parents' San Francisco home. This would go to my sister Margaret and brother-in-law Chris. It would look beautiful in their new home.

The green secretary I had hauled out from our family cabin in the Santa Cruz mountains. This desk with the textured Japanese picture of a boat gently gliding on a river. How many nights as a child I had drifted to sleep, lulled by the water in that image. This would go to Ellen. Ellen who was my soul supporter, whose laughter could always bring me back to the present moment on this journey with cancer. It would be perfect in her massage office.

Melissa's beautiful table, lovingly fashioned from the most precious of woods. Melissa, whose life was taken so early and whose beauty shone through in her craft. Her table which I used for years as an altar would go to Melissa's sister, Helen.

I had already begun giving other, smaller things away at gift-giving times. Items that were special to me and that I knew would be special to those I gave them to.

It's not that I wanted to die; yet I was certainly preparing to die, get-ting things in order to die. Ellen and I even picked this house think-ing that the huge back room would accommodate a hospital bed if it were needed as the disease progressed. The hospital bed placed so that I could watch the birds feeding from the west window and the rolling hills from the east window. The hospital bed brought in to provide bodily comfort when one goes into a coma before death. I had asked Peggy how I would die, what I could expect to expe-rience as the cancer progressed. I had this question among others on one of my lists. She answered so honestly. I am still grateful for her honesty. I was told that as the cancer progressed and filled my pelvic cavity, the cancer and the accumulating fluids would most likely impact my kidneys and I would go into a coma as my kidneys shut down. I had decided on cremation and was considering first donating my body to University of New Mexico medical school so new doctors could cut me up and maybe learn a thing or two more about ovarian cancer.

I had finally retired. Retired from twenty-four years of teaching children with special needs. Retired, with an unbelievably wondrous send-off. I had felt so fortunate to have found a vocation I truly loved. Work I continued to learn from and grow with over the years. The giving and receiving in beautiful balance. I had worked through my initial and then recurrent chemo treatments with so much support from my coworkers and the families whose children I taught. Yet I felt the change in my focus as I truly got in my mind, and felt in my body, that I would not be here that much longer. I knew it was time to stop teaching.

I had been asked so many times by medical professionals and by others who had cancer how I was "fighting the battle." Everyone expected I would be fighting against cancer. This battle against my "enemy," Cancer. As many times as I was asked this I found that I could never relate to it. My experience was not like this at all. My experience was one of surrender, surrender into healing. I wasn't taking up arms against the enemy, I was letting go into the deepest well of surrender toward healing. I knew true healing could take many forms, and I knew one of those forms was dying.

I really was preparing to die. Affairs in order. No surprises for anyone to take care of after my death. I was doing my best to stay current in my relationships. Giving and receiving incredible outpourings of love and appreciation. Spiritually deepening. And now, no visible cancer.

I think I spent that fall a bit depressed. Depression was new to me so I wasn't really sure at the time. I still functioned OK. I still got up every morning, greeted the day as best I could. But something had shifted inside me with all my preparations for dying. Something was not shifting back with the news of more living and I felt stuck. I felt as if I had a foot in both worlds. One foot in the world of the living and one foot in the world of the dying.

I really thought that I was dying. It's not even that I wanted to die, I was just focused in that direction. The act of shifting that focus is the deepest surrender I have ever experienced. What has been confusing about this is that this is how so many speak when they talk of dying, this deep surrender. I had had many opportunities to be with family members and friends as they died, and I could see how much this passing was just another part of life.

Now, I find myself focused on living and trying to do this with a full embrace. Many times lately, I have fallen short.

I thought that hearing the news of the cancer recurring would be the most difficult transition I would have to make. I had no idea that hearing the news that there was no visible cancer would be more difficult. This was hard for me to admit to myself and it's hard to try putting it into words. I have experienced a death of sorts—a death of many of the ways I have known myself to feel and be. So much has been altered in my life, so many layers stripped away: my health, my body as I have known it, my work in the world, my firm footing on my spiritual path.

It seems a bittersweet surrender, this living in transition. I've lived enough years to know that deeper understanding of this time of transition will come. That in retrospect I will see the many blessings of this challenging time. As for now I take deep breaths. Say a prayer. Cry. Express my loving. Stub my toe. Watch the sunset. Laugh. Feel impatient. Walk in the pinions. Schedule my next Catscan. See a good movie. Feel sadness. Meditate. Pay the bills. Act very silly. Watch the birds feeding. Share deeply with loved ones.

Share mundanely with loved ones. I think it is called living.

It's been almost two months since I wrote this monologue and now, having just found out that the cancer is back, I make the transition from living in limbo to living with cancer. Once Again, I am considering treatment options. It is also a challenging time.

Ellen left me a card on the kitchen counter soon after I got the news that the cancer had returned. The message touched me deeply and I wanted to share it with you.

The card had the image of a snowy egret just beginning its flight from a pool of water, the bird's wings not yet fully outstretched. The inscription below read:

> *When you come to the edge of all that you know,*
> *You must believe in one of two things,*
> *There will be earth upon which to stand*
> *or you will be given wings*

(Author Unknown)

KATHLEEN AND A NECTARINE, BOTH IN THE IMAGE OF GOD

Michael Burt

In March 2000 I was treated at the Arizona Cancer Center in Tucson for an aggressive form of lymphoma; high doses of chemotherapy and high doses of radiation were followed by a bone marrow transplant. Typical side effects are fatigue, infection, nausea, mouth sores, vomiting and hair loss. More serious side effects can be fatal.

One day in particular I vomited from morning until night. I had something called breakthrough vomiting that no medication could control. I sat in the middle of my hospital room, vomiting into a pan on the floor. I remember feeling that if I threw up just once more, my skeleton would turn inside out; a little like those old cartoons where the cat eats the fish and then pulls the skeleton out of his mouth.

Now, here is the picture: I am practically doubled over in a chair with my head close to the pan. I am ashen and bald, with several pumps on my IV pole pushing anti-nausea drugs into the catheter dangling from my chest. There is vomit on one of my Birkenstocks.

And then, one of the floor nurses comes in to untangle my IV lines. I am so sick and weak, I can barely raise my head, but I manage. And from how I am doubled over, I am staring at one of the most beautiful asses I've ever seen—an ass as shapely and perfect as a nectarine made personally by God Herself.

The nurse finishes untangling the lines, resets the computers and walks out. I never saw her face. What touched me when I was so sick? What reached me in a way no prayer ever has? I think it was grace—oddly, the grace of a beautiful ass and right in my face. I knew from that moment I was going to be OK.

I am lucky that I have known the grace of another nurse, as well—my wife, Kathleen—whose face I do know. Kathleen and I have been together since long before the cancer, since those days when we were on fire and couldn't get enough of each other. Through the wow of we're having a baby. Through biopsy and diagnosis, chemotherapy, remission, the birth of our son, relapse, surgery, transplant, and remission again.

Two months after our son, Jake, was conceived, I was in the hospital for the biopsy that would reveal the cancer. My grief, guilt and confusion were unbearable. Kathleen stood at the foot of the gurney while the anesthesiologist got the IV started. Looking at her kept me from going crazy. I'm an articulate guy; I'm never speechless—but I still don't know what to make of that feeling. I don't think I have ever been so completely exposed, or so completely accepted.

In the movie *Dead Man Walking*, while Matthew Poncelet was being executed, he kept his gaze on Sister Helen to keep *him* steady on the worst day of his life. That's what it felt like to me before the biopsy; I never needed another soul in my life like I needed Kathleen at that moment.

Whenever I come to die, I will take that vision of Kathleen with me into the next life: Kathleen, my beautiful, soulful, radiant, pregnant friend and lover. And I will add to that the sound of Jake's bare feet as he runs on the hardwood floors in our house.

Through the dark world of my cancer; the grief and guilt and pain and despair. Through the lost and lonely nights of my lost and lonely soul, Kathleen was there.

She held me through a thousand hours of pain and fear. She cried with me when the news was bad, and cried with me when the news was good.

And, I am sorry to say, I have brought sorrow to her. There have been times when I have gone away from her. Not only because I didn't have the physical energy to participate in my life, but cancer is such an emotional albatross and it is always there *even when it is gone.*

I wonder if other illnesses are like this. Cancer is like dog shit on the sole of your shoe. You can *never* get rid of the smell, even if you scrape and scrape and walk blocks away from the pile you stepped in. Never. Grief lasts a lifetime; we may get comfortable with it, but it never goes away. *Never. Never. Never. Never. Never.*

My cancer and maybe my death. This is my poem about all of it; it's called "Radiation Therapy":

> *Sandbags to hold me*
> *In the focused deadly ray.*
> *No one wants to die here,*
> *A mummy on display.*
> *Who is here to touch me?*
> *No one in the room;*
> *Buried in a leaded vault,*
> *A radiation tomb.*
>
> *Saviors come though gloved and masked*
> *To turn me in my place;*
> *Basting me through leaded doors,*
> *Then cooking me from legs to face.*
> *Cook his spine, his heart, his brain*
> *To just a medium rare.*
> *Serve him on a china plate*
> *With parsley everywhere.*

The doctor comes with sterile fork
To check if I am done.
A thousand questions on my lips;
I see he has to run.
Technicians hold their forks and knives,
They serve a subtle wine.
In dreams I hold my wife and son;
The staff begins to dine.

The Christ comes in unmasked, ungloved.
Can this be how He shows His love?
Another patient at the door.
My bones are scattered on the floor.

When Kathleen and I became lovers, she said something to me that I had never heard before; something very sexy and very earthy. I am not going to share those words with you, but I want to tell you that they are never far from me and I think of them in the most unlikely situations—like this one.

Kathleen, I love you so much. Life has broken our hearts. But it has also given us Jake. The best I can hope for him is that someday he will meet an authentic beauty like you who loves him the way you have loved me.

Lena Albert

*Dedicated to my father, Hy Albert,
and to the memory of Lynne Higdon*

OK, here's the question: Suppose you just got a new Harley, totally customized for you. I ask you to take me to Mesa Verde—only I don't know how to get there and neither do you. What will you do? This is a question I used to ask my students when I was a studies skills teacher at the community college. Answer, obviously, get a map. Well, there is no map for the journey I went on.

I remember my diagnosis. The doctor didn't call me when she said she would. I called the office and was told that she was on vacation. What? What do you mean? She was supposed to call me with the results of my biopsy. One moment. The doctor gets on the phone. The biopsy is positive. You have breast cancer. Make an appointment with me in two weeks when I get back. How can you just leave me hanging? I am totally unprepared for this. Well, you'll need a lumpectomy, chemotherapy and radiation. That's the usual course of treatment. Goodbye. Click. I stare at the receiver in shock. This can't be. What am I going to do? There I am abandoned and afraid.

I call my closest friend, Paula. Hello, Paula? I can't believe what just happened. The biopsy, it was positive. I have breast cancer. I'm in shock. Silence. Is she there? How are you, Paula? I never heard from her again.

I am left standing alone in my kitchen. No support. Helpless. Oh

God, please help me. Oh my God, my God, save me, strengthen me. There is an ache deep in my heart. I feel myself contracting, being pulled down by a fierce whirlpool. I'm panicked. It feels like I am drowning in the middle of the deepest part of the ocean with no life preserver, nothing familiar to hold on to. The whirling mass of water is sucking me toward its center of darkness. Like Jonah, I am swallowed into the belly of the whale. Would I be spit out across the water to the safety of dry land? Would I drift for a while with my head above water? Where is that map?

I ask my friends to join me in a hair-cutting ceremony. I am taking control of this. My hair is not going to fall out on my pillow one morning or drop off my head when I am taking a shower. Marianne: *I'll have to think about this. I'll let you know.* Susan: *Gasp.* Charlene: *What a great idea! I'd be honored to share that experience with you.* Joyce: *I'll do that for you.* Do that for me? What about doing that with me? Come over here and walk with me. They all did. Losing my hair was the least of it. I saved my hair from that ceremony and when all of my treatments were finished I went to Central Park and released my hair to the trees, the bushes and the birds in Strawberry Fields.

With cancer comes the denial: this can't be happening to me. Cancer is deceptive and deceiving. It is quiet as it lies in wait to attack by surprise. Then the regimen begins. I discover that the treatment is worse than the disease. I won't die from cancer, it is the chemotherapy that will kill me.

Having breast cancer is like being inaugurated into a club that nobody wants to belong to. Members eat at the banquet of life and death. They learn to dance to an undefinable new rhythm. There are no dues if you don't include the exorbitant medical bills. No one who joins is ever the same.

There are no answers. There is no wrong path. I drew my own map and went on my own personal journey. My questions guide me: How is God running through my body? How do I pray when I'm too sick to try? How do I go through this with dignity? How do I suffer without adding to my suffering? How do I use all that is given to me to step deeper into love and compassion for myself and others? How can I still be in the world in the best way I can?

The night before my lumpectomy I took a knife and had a private ceremony with myself. I hold the knife. I decide what to cut out. I challenge myself to cut into my interior and release all that does not belong. I cut out self-hatred. I cut out that which makes me small. I cut out all that narrows my view of myself. I cut out the patterns that created cancer. I cut away all that is not my authentic self. I choose life as sung by Frank Sinatra: My Way.

The doctor said the surgery would be a slam dunk. In other words, remove the lump and there will be no spread. It was not a slam dunk. The cancer had spread to the lymph nodes. Here's a question: What happens to the breast once it has been surgically removed? When you die you are put in a box and buried in Mother Earth or your ashes are spread over land and water. What happens to the breast that has been lopped off? Does it get thrown in the garbage—part of hospital waste? Is there a breast cemetery that no one knows about?

Chemotherapy was like being a boxer in the middle of the ring. Each round of drugs knocked me off my feet only to get up again and receive another punch. With each chemotherapy treatment I experienced a loss of my sense of self. This disconnection extended to my family and friends. I felt like an alien in my own body. I could feel the chemotherapy in my head and my brain felt cold. Through my pain and tears I could not feel God with me. I lost my sense of meaning and purpose. I felt insecure, unloved, and unwanted. My only escape was sleep and television. This was the dark night of my soul. It was Persephone's journey into Hades. My sense of who I am and the familiar landmarks of my life were sacrificed as I was brought down and into my essence. Life as I knew it was completely shattered. I learned that courage does not mean being unafraid but comes as I keep on in the face of my fears.

Radiation. I felt like a piece of meat. Technicians touching my breast, measuring my breast with cold instruments, marking it with felt-tipped pens, talking to the back of my head, not introducing themselves to me even though I asked them to. I was an object. I felt demeaned, violated by unwanted fingers touching my body. I was bald, no hair on any part of my body, not even a hair in my nose. I was skinny and pale. I lay down on my stomach so that my breast hung through an opening—it was like being in a magician's box without the magic.

I decided to be blessed by my own radiance. My friend Lisa invited me to attend a healing circle at Temple Ansche Chesed on the Upper West Side in Manhattan. During the service a prayer was read that included the words, *My God, the soul you have placed in me is pure. You it was who created it. You formed it. You blew it into me.* I couldn't control the tears that streamed down my cheeks. That's it! That is how God is running through my body. I received the awareness of the sacredness of the breath. Breathing itself is a testament to God's presence in me. In this place of grace I can spread my wings and fly free in the spaciousness that is God's love.

I did not choose this illness but it is now a part of my life's story. What I thought was important is no longer of value—how I look, how much money I have, how successful I am, what people say about me. When everything was stripped away the one thing I had left was my soul. It is my soul that matters most.

Do you like amusement parks, roller coasters? If you want the ride of your life, get cancer. You will have more ups and downs than you will ever know what to do with. It has everything: adventure, crisis, intermission. And you don't have to buy a ticket. Check your breast pocket or maybe your lungs or colon or your prostate. It could be hiding anywhere. But remember you can't get off.

I'm not a roller coaster person. I was forced to take this ride. But I wouldn't change it for anything. I think the main thing is allowing myself to go through this experience and to feel every single bit of it. I let myself go through the not knowing, the uncertainties, the fears, the rage, to feel it all. Physically it felt like some fabric or fiber was being rewoven. I felt like there was a big hole where something had dropped out and then there was this reweaving of fiber in places I thought were untouchable inside me. And all of a sudden there was immense light.

More than anything my joy comes from a sense of connection. I can't say it's just with God. It's a moment of total connection where there is not a sense of where I end and begin, and there is such an incredible vibrancy and awakeness. My capacity for joy and delighting in every moment has deepened because I know at an instant it can be taken away. And I learned that there is nothing constant but change.

How do I remain present in the face of suffering? I take a breath, I meditate, I become still and go in deeply with remembering all that I have learned, just remembering. Destiny asked me to remap the familiar boundaries of my inner landscape and expand into wider and new territories. My soul was my compass. I was driven by a powerful longing. I found a place of love and mercy—and compassion. One thing I know for sure is that each moment is holy. Come, put one foot solidly in front of the other and breathe with me.

SISTERS, FACE TO FACE

Pamela Avis

I stepped off the train at three a.m. Downtown Cleveland, mid-January is cold—very cold. I had two huge bags, bulging black canvas pieces of luggage. I pulled them off the train, turned and searched the distant parking lot for my sister, Kris. I saw her car, grabbed the handles of my baggage, and pulling them behind me I walked toward where she was parked. The luggage wheels rumbled and grumbled as I walked over the rough sidewalk, and they bounced across the second set of train tracks. As I neared her she got out of the car and waited for me. It had been over a year since we'd seen each other and my first sight of her face chilled me. Cold dread settled into my heart as my imagination showed me a vision of what might lie ahead. We hugged each other closely.

Kris had called me a few weeks prior to my arrival in Cleveland and asked the question I had hoped never to hear, "Can you come stay with me?" Her voice, her attitude, were bright and upbeat—her usual—with no hint of how she felt or what was happening in her body. But I knew that she wouldn't have asked me to come if she had been able to continue caring for herself and her six-year-old son, Joshua. I didn't want to be fearful, but I was. I had never been very good at living within the mystery of life, and I didn't have a clue about what I would need to face in the weeks ahead.

One evening, after I had been with her about a month, we were in her bathroom. I was sitting on the edge of her big Jacuzzi tub and she was standing in front of the vanity staring at her reflection in the mirror. I looked at her standing there, wearing only a camisole top. She was beyond thin—skin and bones. It had been three years since the diagnosis of breast cancer. She had declined surgery, deciding to seek other forms of treatment. The attack on her body had continued. Good cells were gobbled up leaving the left side of her body scarred and mutilated and the left side of her face distorted from nerve damage. It was as if Darth Vader and the dark Force had invaded her being. The Death Star had been fired. The monstrous seeds of domination had spread through her skin—her bones—her muscles—her organs—her brain. All the different treatments she had tried had not found her Luke Skywalker—her destroyer of the evil empire of cancer.

As she looked at herself she reached into a drawer and pulled out a picture of a model in a bikini on a beach somewhere. "When I get better, that's how I'll look," she said. "I've lost all the fat. I'll go to Saint-Tropez and get a tan. With my blonde hair I'll have all the men looking at me. That's how I'll look." She stared at the picture and her reflection for a few moments and then turned to me and asked, "Remember that card I gave you for your birthday, the one of the four women cartoon characters? I labeled them, remember? You were the one with HIPS TOO LARGE. Joan was the one with THIGHS TOO LARGE. Dee was the one with BREASTS TOO SMALL. And I was the one with FACE POORLY DRAWN. See, Face Poorly Drawn. And I have no ass—it's all gone. Poorly drawn face and no ass!" And she laughed and I laughed until our sides and our stomachs hurt. We laughed because we couldn't cry. Crying would have shattered the illusion that we were not in the dance with death and so the tears and the sadness stayed hidden.

I struggled daily to understand my role in this battle. When I used words like that with her—battle—struggle—war—she would shake her head, look at me sadly and say that her answer was to love her disease, to transform it with love and blessings, and that I needed to do the same. I tried.

One weekend she had friends visiting from out of town. Joshua was at his dad's and so I was sleeping in his room, the room next to Kris's. I awoke around two a.m. and heard her crying. I went to her door and knocked. She told me to come in and I opened the door. She was pacing from one end of the room to the other, holding an icebag to her side and crying hysterically. Her face a twisted mask of pain, the look of fear so primal I couldn't even imagine what she was going through. All I could do was stand in one place and stay present. She kept asking questions—*why I am going through this—what does God want of me—when is it going to end?* "Oh, Pammie, I can't stand it anymore. I can't stand this pain anymore. What's the point of all this?" And she stared at me as if expecting an answer. "I don't know, Krissie," I said. "I don't know what it's about. I don't understand, either. Is there anything I can do for you? Yes, I can hold you." I put my arms around her and held her as gently as I could— and she rested her head against my chest. We stood like that for a long time. Eventually, the pain subsided enough for her to lie down on her bed and drift off to sleep. It was a terrible night for me.

The next morning she got up and prepared to go to church, acting as if the scene of the night before had not happened. She dressed and did her hair and put on makeup. Her friends were leaving and she was bright and cheery as they hugged her and said their good-byes. Once they were out the door she collapsed into the deck chair by the window overlooking her patio. She sat there with the sun coming in to warm her, covered with a blue fleece blanket, and she fell asleep.

Later that day after she had awakened I fixed her something to eat. I remarked that I was glad she'd been able to rest after the hell she'd just been through. She turned to me, her face hard, and she said, "How dare you judge my life—you don't know anything about my life. My life hasn't been hell. Everybody is always judging me, and I am sick of it." No amount of explaining made any difference. The fact that I had been speaking of the night before wasn't heard. What

I had seen, her pain so visible, her distress and agony so obvious, seemed like a form of hell to me. I said that to her and she replied, "You shouldn't be so judgmental, Pam. It's only pain, you know. It's only pain." The conversation was closed. I knew that even though her anger was directed at me it wasn't about me at all.

She died a few months later. For the last three days of her life she sat up straight in her bed and gazed into a place I couldn't go. I don't know who she saw there or who greeted her—who helped prepare her for her passing over—but whoever they were, they seemed to bring her peace. She died shortly after seven a.m. on Wednesday, May 12, 1999, with me on one side and our father on the other side. My dad and I each held a hand as her breathing just stopped and she was gone. We sat in the silence and said our good-byes.

She left behind her young son, a father, a stepmother, three sisters, one brother, eleven nieces and nephews, and many friends.

In the Beginning

Jennie Reasoner-Wagner

This is a part of the story of a life—mine—and what happened when I found out I had breast cancer. Cancer is a disease of chaos and disorder that would surround me with chaos and disorder for over a year. I would hate it so much.

The story begins with finding a lump and it should end with the party I gave at the end of the treatment ordeal a year and a half later. It doesn't. There are now regular followup visits to the oncologist. I am always reminded IT could happen again. It seems that you can survive cancer, but you can never really be cured.

I am very glad to be alive.

April 23:

During the shower, to avoid thinking of the lump, this new part of me I have just discovered, I tried to decide on the perfect outfit for dinner out with friends tonight: black velvet leggings, a long silvery sweater and black suede boots.

It is not a large lump, but it is a bit bigger than the one I found three years ago. That one drained in less than two minutes at the doctor's office—an event hardly worth mentioning. And even though this lump is larger and I have a funny feeling about it, there is really no reason to worry. It will probably turn out to be just another cyst caused from too much caffeine. I will just quit drinking Diet Cokes for a while. No woman in my family has ever had breast cancer. I am not even old enough for a mammogram. You have to be older than thirty-seven to have breast cancer. Don't you?

Besides, this lump is not *that* large. I try to make it smaller with my thoughts, an easy enough mental exercise. I picture a large wall, plastered white and smooth. A lump like mine would never be noticed there. No one would see this lump in the corrugated bed of an old Dodge club-cab pickup. Who could see it among all the bangs, dings and empty beer cans? These are calming thoughts. *I will not touch the lump again.*

My eyes go back and forth from my breast to the wall above the tiled shower. There are little blobs of mildew near the ceiling that are much bigger than this thing beneath my skin seems to be, this thing that just suddenly appeared tonight. It gives me great comfort to remember that sometimes days go by without me even noticing the mildew spots above me.

The bathroom is the only room in my house where I have never cried. I want to keep it that way.

I turn my right side directly into the shower and wait until the hot water runs out, fighting to keep my promise not to touch the lump. I lose the fight. I touch the place again. It is still there, undissolved and hidden under my skin. I try to push the thing back into my flesh until my fingers cramp, while the running water turns warm, tepid, cool and then cold.

MAY 2:

Malignant: *(adjective) (pathological)* "Tending to produce death." From "to act maliciously." Synonyms: malevolent, malicious, mean, spiteful, venomous, deadly, lethal, poisonous, toxic.

I bought my first pair of red cowboy boots last week in El Paso before all of this. I have wanted red cowboy boots since I was ten years old. Now I have red cowboy boots and I wore them when I saw the surgeon for the first time.

My legs are slim and red leather this afternoon. I have on my favorite long yellow sweater. My hair is long too, curly, shiny and red—like the boots I am wearing. It swings around my shoulders when I walk. I am wearing the boots for luck but I don't think I need luck today. Right now, I remember thinking as I saw my reflection in the glass door of the medical building, what I really need is a white silk shirt to tuck in the jeans.

May 5:

Today is the second time I have seen the surgeon. I went to outpatient surgery wearing gray sweats and Reeboks. In a little room I am given a green cotton surgical wrapper. After that I waited for forty-five minutes in the green recliner until two nurses came for me.

They wheeled me through two green hallways. The operating room is green too, very cold and green. The whole hospital is green, green, green.

I wanted to stay awake. I wanted to watch. They let me.

So I watched the surgeon's eyes through the procedure. He is probably a bad poker player with such eyes. They are very clear green (more green) and easy to read.

Last night I made little notes on yellow Post-its and stuck them on my right breast just before I was wheeled into the operating room. One said, "Please use sharp, clean instruments." The nurse removed them without comment and tossed them in a waste can. I had hoped for more. I wanted them to notice how brave and funny I was. How fearless I was.

I watched as the surgeon cut out the lump. He did it quickly. The tumor looked like a peeled blood orange in his latex hands. It was almost as big as my fist.

I tested the surgeon's eyes. I asked him to send the tumor up to pathology. He said he would. Then I knew. And he knew that I knew. The nurse looked at us and then she knew that we both knew. I could go to sleep now.

An hour later, someone is calling my name and waking me up. I complain about having to get dressed again. I was so comfortable curled on the gurney hidden behind green and white curtains, floating around in the cloud of post-surgery wrapped up in a dryer-warmed blanket. A nurse gives me graham crackers and cranberry juice. She helps me with my clothes.

The doctor finally (has it been only an hour?) pushes back the curtain surrounding my gurney.

He says, "You have cancer."

I get up and stumble around trying to gather my belongings and my thoughts. From out of nowhere, a friend appears and begins gathering the prescriptions for painkillers, post-surgical instruction papers, pamphlets on all sorts of cancer treatment and referrals to specialists. He stuffs them in his pants pockets. Some of them stick out like the wings of seagulls diving below the water for snacks at the beach. I wonder if I will ever go to the beach again.

Later, two days from now, I will find out that because of this blood-orange thing—this cancer—and because of its size and the violent course of treatment I will have, I will not have hair for nearly a year. I will not have children, ever. I will have no certainty that I will get to keep my breast or my life at this point. The tumor was very large. It had exploded like a dandelion in the wind, scattering glittering cancer cells throughout my body. A lot will depend on my lymph nodes, the extent of their infection, whether they have taken root anywhere else in my body.

Later, three days from now, I will have to make decisions about my treatment. I already know that I will choose the chemo and radiation.

Much later, three weeks from now, yet another person will call me on the phone and ask me to justify these decisions when so many alternative treatments are out there. I will not chew on some exotic tree bark, though, nor will I swallow creosote capsules or chant my sickness away. That just is not my style. I will, though, in a final fit of pique, frustration and nausea tell the next person that this choice of mine comes from a desperate desire, that if I do not survive, I do not want my last words to all those I love to be, "Damn, I wish I'd had that chemo."

Going home from the hospital, I sit sedated and stupid and make a tightly rolled paper tube of the little handouts about chemotherapy and radiation.

Later on, after I am home and in bed, I prop myself up and try to read them. There is a phone on the night table by the bed. I am waiting for it to ring.

I am waiting for the night pathologist (is there such a person?) to call the doctor who will then call me and tell me about the mistake the day pathologist made, that all I had was a benign cyst, that my slide somehow got mixed up with the one for someone who had cancer.

The little booklet about chemotherapy is on the floor. I tossed it there after searching through it for descriptions of the drugs I would be given, though I didn't know their names yet. So I read about each drug that could make me bald and sterile. Then I threw it on the floor.

My red cowboy boots are sitting out by the closet door. After three days they have not been put away. This is just the beginning of disorder.

And they do not look lucky. They look like red cowboy boots.

A Doctor's Journey

Janet Greene, M.D.

I never intended to be a doctor. No one on either side of my family was in the medical profession and I never gave it a thought
until a back injury ended my possibility of teaching physical
education. I believed in medicine in my core, having been a sickly
child and an asthmatic. I depended on medication to keep me alive
my entire life. Expecting, in the back of my mind, that doctors
would always be there to take care of me, I felt safe in the world.

When I became a doctor, I realized that this sense of security was
unfounded, but I still trusted medicine. I knew nothing of comple-
mentary medicine (and was actually resistant to knowing more
about natural healing), but I was forced to consider these modali-
ties when my former spiritual teacher refused to allow me to practice that "barbaric" kind of medicine on him. This put me in a rather
awkward position since I was the only doctor he or any of the others in this particular spiritual community depended on for their care.
It was through his rejection of Western medicine that I discovered a
whole new world of healing, but even then, if *I* got sick I used
antibiotics. I was deeply afraid not to. Medicine breathed for me;
kept me alive.

Because of a lifetime of asthma, I had a horrible fear that I would
not live through cancer surgery, not because of the actual operation,
but because of the anesthesia. I had been taught that asthmatics
required more anesthesia than others to help relax the lungs and
prevent bronchospasm. In my mind, I translated this into a fear of
being overanesthetized. I had ten days to prepare for what I thought
would be my final days; saying my goodbyes, fully expecting never
to awaken. The prospect of someone putting me "out" struck fear

into one of the deepest places I have ever known. The very thought of it made me feel as if my heart would simply stop in my chest.

At the time of surgery, I wasn't aware of moving from the stretcher onto the operating table, although the nurses told me later I had done it myself. I'm glad I was unconscious, because I didn't want to see that cold, sterile room that I remembered from my days as a medical student. At the time I had assisted on so many surgeries. I never understood how people were so willing to go like sheep to slaughter, lights out without a fight, seemingly unafraid. I knew back then what a crisis the prospect of surgery triggered in me and projected this feeling onto everyone.

After two and a half years, I still get anxious in the quiet hours of the night when I "remember" the surgery; a stranger tearing my body apart, ripping out my uterus and then discovering that lesion on my left ovary. And the pain. I can *still* feel the pain. I couldn't believe they cut this beautiful body in half, sliced and diced it, my guts out on the table like a string of raw sausage.

I remember when I loved my body above all things. I was so proud of my athleticism, my muscles, my ability to run faster and jump higher than anyone else, to swim under the waves and the blue shimmering water of the pool. I remember how whole I felt swimming and the stillness under the water, the oneness with myself and the universe, the quiet. And I also remember the leaf floating on top of the water, dying. The last leaf I would hold from my mother's house, as she lay dying of cancer.

Prior to my surgery, I had asked the doctor to reassure me during the operation, that it was going okay, that I would live through it. With my surgical experience, I knew I would hear him in spite of my unconsciousness. He understood I would hear the classical music I chose and even asked me what I wanted to listen to. I had made one request: "Please tell me that I am going to wake up!" He didn't. I believe he never told me because of his own fear when he saw that tainted ovary and knew this was no longer a simple endometrial cancer. He told me later that he *couldn't* tell me I was all right, because in *his* mind I wasn't. I know in my heart my recovery was prolonged because I didn't get the reassurance that I was going to live through the surgery.

When I went to the hospital for the surgery, I was an emotional wreck. I could hardly talk and was doing my best to just get to my room when suddenly, over the door, I encountered the words, ONCOLOGY WARD. That was when I lost it. I wept for hours. These words completely pulled the rug out from under me and left me with a sense of overwhelming doom. I didn't understand how the people who designed this could hospital be so insensitive.

Because of all this, I am a very different doctor today. I thought I understood the dying patient before. I had dealt so much with death and dying, especially in my years as an emergency room physician in New York and in my spiritual practice, that of Tibetan Buddhism, which focuses on death, dying, suffering and compassion. But nothing prepared me for this, for the complexity of the mental and physical processes, the nightmare of dealing with a medical system that was not compassionate and did not serve me as a cancer patient. My doctor was not in touch with how deeply my fear ran and how devastating this news was when he said the words "You have cancer." In my opinion, there are many big problems with medicine, but it was the little things that were so affecting when I was in such a vulnerable state.

There is nothing "cookbook" about cancer, and yet the treatments are cookbook medicine. I had the choice of doing chemotherapy and decided to use alternative methods instead, after weeks of agonizing internal debate and insensitive bludgeoning from one of my doctors. This doctor, who I went to for help, took away my hope. That was my decision, and I will live or die by it, but I take full responsibility and know it was the right decision at the time. As a result of having to deal with that, I am a changed human being, and a better doctor. Without fear, I can support my patients' decisions about their own lives, as I have realized how completely personal and extraordinary each person's journey is.

In spite of the difficulty of the cancer experience, I have found it to be a blessing because of what I was forced to confront and transform. I am especially gratified when I remember the kind of doctor I used to be.

Swimming to the Surface

Willow Rose

It all starts with nausea. Life begins and feels like it's ending with nausea. I started throwing up at midnight on the first day I had chemotherapy. The doctor was so surprised, he said, "Already? That's early." Kneeling on the cotton shag rug, gripping the cold white porcelain, confined in the tiny cave-like closet that houses the toilet, I felt scared and lonely and little, as the walls closed in around me.

The smell of my vomit rose up to meet me and my intestines ached as I emptied everything within. I feared I would start throwing up pieces of myself and maybe I did, since I now feel I have lost who I was down that toilet. She's been flushed away with the vomit and I have nothing else to do but start over.

Repeated late-night calls over several days to whatever oncologist was on call from my doctor's group finally yielded the right combination of drugs to control the vomiting. Marinol and Decadron in the morning, Marinol and Decadron in the afternoon, Marinol and Ativan (aahh) in the evening. But deep wrenching dry heaves went on for five days after each chemo treatment.

So I continued to lose myself in the toilet, flushing pieces of who I used to be away with the nothingness, the air, the energy expended. Who am I now? What do I grab onto? No longer the porcelain sides of the bowl, but air. I grab pieces of myself out of the air. I plant seeds of myself to grow again. What will they manifest? Who will I be? How do I manifest the patience to wait and see what grows?

Who am I? Who am I? Who am I? Am I a woman or a ten-year-old?

Since the mastectomy I have one side of each on my chest. But ten-year-olds don't usually have ten-inch scars across their chest—so…I'm a woman with a scar across her chest.

I miss my boob. I thought she was cute. I lost the perky one. I've seen pictures of women who have gotten tattoos across their scar, empowering symbols of growth and strength like trees and dragons.

The tattoo I'd really like to get on my chest is a topographical map. It would look just like my missing breast did—only much flatter. Concentric circles would define the old perimeter, while lines closer together would indicate a steep elevation and lines farther apart, a gradual slope. Then a lover would know exactly what territory she was about to embark upon.

Of course this is just pretend, because who cares if there's a boob there. I'm here! But what does it mean to be here when I've been so far away? Where do I go to find out? I find myself searching the past to find my future.

I can remember when I first learned to swim. It was at day camp and I was so proud of myself. "Mommy, Daddy, look at me! Look what I learned today!" It seemed like I had always been in the water and always would be. If my legs grew together into a tail, and all of a sudden I grew gills in the side of my neck, that would be all right. I never wanted to get out of the water. Swimming across lakes from one shore to the other excited me the most. The first time was at the lake in Maine where my family vacationed.

In the cool, early dawn, with the mist rising all around him, my father would go out in a canoe to take home movies of the loons that lived there. But midday, as I glide through the sparkling water, the mysterious loons with their haunting calls are in hiding.

Stopping in the middle to tread water I see the shore ahead of me and the shore behind me, so tiny and far away, just a bright colored line, nothing more.

The lake is deep and dark below my bobbing head but supportive and nurturing like a womb. Around me gentle ripples in constant motion glisten in the bright sun. I feel blissfully happy. Floating on my back, I feel my body rise and fall with the lake's motion, rise and fall with my breath, until it is the same motion. We are breathing together, the lake and I. I hear a sound—a deep echoing, pulsating hum—the sound of the lake. It vibrates my body. I am a welcomed part of the water's universe. A universe of love, a universe of perfect completeness.

The memory of this perfect completeness inspires me, encourages me, gives me something to grasp onto when I wonder how am I ever going to feel comfortable in my body again.

My tired body with its new geography, a disrupted landscape that it is difficult to get used to. In the site of my surgery I have feelings of tightness and numbness that may always be there, that may never leave, that don't greatly restrict my movement but are a constant reminder that something catastrophic happened there.

To turn catastrophe into healing, to grow new vegetation on the slope of a lava flow, to rebuild a structure from the rubble of an earthquake, this is my task after almost a year of cancer treatment that included surgery, chemotherapy and radiation.

I survived by hiding deep inside myself, and rarely letting feelings and emotions rise to the surface. Getting through every day one by one was my only goal then, a plant in dormancy, conserving my strength for the day in the future when blooming would once again be possible.

THE OTHER PATIENT

Dedre Umoja Will

It is cancer. The doctor's voice was flat, no emotion. My worst fears have been confirmed. "She'll need to come in for a follow-up tomorrow." No response from me. The handset rattled back onto the cradle. I sat in my study feeling numb, except for a pain in my heart. I will never forget the wave of feelings that swept over me, panic, fear, shock, despair.

Then came the tears, then came the trembling; and sobs. How long I sat there, I don't remember. Willow called home. Her voice was shaking, and small. I did not tell her the doctor had told me. I wanted her to come home to me. I wanted to take her into my arms and just hold her, without ever letting go. "I will be here waiting for you," I said. She spoke some words that I did not hear as I choked back the tears…when I hung up the phone, more tears, shaking, becoming uncontrollable, followed by a time of silence.

I called them one by one. It is cancer. It is cancer. It is cancer.

I called Kris. She said, in a gentle voice, "I'll be right there." I went downstairs and opened the door. She embraced my tears, held me and rocked me, until I was quiet.

Our dear Kris, she came and she never left. I had no idea that day how I would wake up again and face life tomorrow. But one act of love carried me, and us, through that day, and the surgery, and the chemotherapies, and those gray days when all we could do was cry.

Six months before the diagnosis, when we moved into a new home, we had no idea there would be an angel next door. In this journey, each day, each moment becomes more precious. Every dream is a prayer; every act of kindness is hope. I think of other angels who arrived, who guarded us and stood by our side. I think of them with fond remembrance and thanksgiving for their gifts.

Women fall in love with women. I remember the first time I saw her. It was on Thanksgiving Day, ten years ago. I'll never forget that day, when two souls meet, and discover that they are kindred spirits.

Willow is the love I sought and dreamed of knowing someday in my life. Now that I found her, I'm not ready for this dream to end. She tells me that I am her best friend. She calls me destiny, and her soul mate. Well, in the same breath, let me tell you, she is all these things to me.

Imagine waking up one day and knowing your whole world has changed. Suddenly Willow and I faced each other, not knowing what could unfold. You want to cling to the way life was before, knowing that there are no choices left, except surrender, let go of control, let go.

There were times when I felt helpless, and exhausted, and terrified by what our lives had become, while I watched over Willow during the chemotherapy treatments, and during the radiation, seeing her fear, holding her when she was fragile.

Sometimes I cannot let go of anger. Why me? I must have asked this question a thousand times. Why us? Why Willow? God, I don't want Willow to die! I want her to live. I want us to live and love and be together, old and gray, and dancing, and I will pray to the goddesses: Send your magic. Transform our tears and make them a potion of fortune.

I experienced enormous grief and depression when I found myself abandoned by people I believed were both our friends, people who told me in no uncertain words that they would support Willow but not me. Already feeling the possibility of losing the most important person in my life, and facing such fear and unknowingness about the future, I found myself abandoned to tears and disbelief that people could be so insensitive and hurtful.

Willow is not the only patient. Willow and I are one. It is not possible to take care of one of us without taking care of the other, but they left, one by one. It is especially difficult for me to understand how anyone would choose to abandon us during the most challenging and difficult moments imaginable. I felt betrayed, and I cannot deny the anger I felt about this, and the sorrow. It made me redefine what a friend is.

Willow and I have carried on. We understand who our family, friends and support people are, and we can lean on them when we are tired, or afraid, or need strength, and we know we can lean on each other.

There are many lessons life teaches us, and these lessons, and the challenges—never giving up on the power of love and prayer, not fearing the outcome, living in the moment, being courageous even when death seems an inevitable possibility—can become some of life's great blessings. Our love has become more meaningful, and among the lessons I have learned with Willow, I have learned never to give up.

I dedicate this poem with all my love to Willow:

> *As I traveled to find*
> *peace of mind*
> *I found along life's road*
> *love that would stay*
> *until we reach*
> *the end of our days*

Sharing our dreams
making our journey
to where destiny leads
and we are not alone
as we walk together
with the gentle hands of angels
on our shoulders.

LEAVING

Deborah Gunderman

How do you know when it is time to leave? Leave your family, leave a job, leave town, leave a lover, leave a friend, leave a home, leave a community you have known for many years, leave your body, leave your life? I don't know. I just know I had to leave. It was a difficult choice to make—to stay near the friends who loved me, supported me and carried me through my experience with cancer or move away in order to save my life.

How could I leave my dear friend Ruth? We have known each other for nine years and she has been like a soul sister to me. When we met, our lives seemed to mirror one another. We were both divorced, no children except for our pets, no special men in our lives. We both loved music and art and doing things spontaneously. We became fast friends. In fact Ruth showed me the true meaning of friendship. She has given me her time, her love, her attention. She remembers things like my birthday and recently called me to wish me well on the morning I started my new job. Without hesitation and without my asking, Ruth planned to be with me the day of my initial surgery for cancer. It was Monday, October 13, 1997. She picked me up early that morning and drove me to the hospital. She stayed with me until they wheeled me to surgery. She was the first person I saw when I came out of anesthesia. She had been there all day. When I came home, she picked up medicines, shopped for groceries and talked to me every day.

Ruth and I had season tickets to the Dallas Symphony Orchestra. I'll never forget the first performance we attended after I started radiation. It was Mahler's Symphony no. 3. Parking for the symphony center was underground. Our seats were at the top of the balcony.

To get from the parking lot to the balcony meant climbing five steep flights of stairs. I was too exhausted to make the climb so we took the elevator. Once off the elevator, we laughed about how we could see ourselves years later as little old ladies still attending the symphony together and having no choice but to use the elevators. By the next performance, I gave it my all and climbed those five steep flights of stairs. It was sweet victory.

Radiation treatments began on November 11, 1997, about one month after the surgery. I was scheduled to receive twenty-nine treatments to my pelvic and abdominal area—five days a week for almost six weeks. I already had plans to fly to Phoenix at Christmas to be with my dad. Spending Christmas in Arizona had become a tradition since my divorce. This year it was especially important. The trip became my goal, my light at the end of the tunnel, what would get me through radiation. I did not give the radiologist an option. I was leaving town for Christmas! By the time Christmas arrived, I was dehydrated, fatigued and had diarrhea every day. I went to Phoenix anyway. I'll never regret the effort it took to make that trip.

The serendipitous events throughout this journey with cancer have been the most meaningful to me. Early in 1997, I decided to create a workshop for women about feminine wisdom. I was working again as an independent management consultant and trainer. Having recently left full-time employment with two large consulting firms, I had become increasingly discouraged about how the wisdom of women was not valued in the workplace. About this same time, I clearly remember saying to myself, "I am not well." Later in the year, I would know what that meant.

After several consultations with a business friend, I designed the workshop and sent out the announcement. I was also seeing my gynecologist about my health concerns. A lump was removed from the scar tissue left from my hysterectomy in 1992. The pathology report suggested that I had a cancer called low-grade endometrial stromal sarcoma. I was in shock. My mother had died from breast cancer five years before. I might have expected breast cancer. I never expected this.

The pathologist sent the slides to a gynecological pathology specialist in Dallas for a second opinion. All I could do was wait. In the meantime, I began receiving registrations for the workshop from women I had known over the years and some I hadn't. The second opinion came back as a sixty percent probability of cancer. The slides and report were sent for a final opinion to a pathology specialist at Harvard Medical School in Boston. My case was considered unique.

The wait continued. I pushed the thought of cancer aside to conduct the workshop. Twenty-five women attended. We shared personal stories about our lives and the special wisdom we have as women. We laughed and cried together. It was such a wonderful day that we agreed to meet every two months and have done so now for over four years.

This group of women became a tremendous source of support to me just when I needed it the most. The final opinion agreed with the diagnosis of cancer. I was to begin treatment right away. This group of wise women planned to pray for me at eight a.m. the day of my surgery. Ruth and I were at the hospital, chatting and waiting for me to go to surgery, when suddenly we both felt a peaceful presence move through the room. We looked at the clock. It was eight a.m. From that point on, I had no doubt that I was being cared for. About a month after completing radiation, I needed emergency surgery. The treatments had damaged my small intestines and caused a partial collapse. My friend Sue came to the hospital to be with me this time. Nine days later when I was released, Sue came to my home, did my laundry and vacuumed the carpet. More importantly, she stayed and talked.

As my strength slowly returned and I tried to pull my life together, I looked for ways to counter the many damaging effects of radiation and surgery. I worked with a Pilates instructor, an acupuncturist and a naturopath. My dreams encouraged me to consider the deeper meaning of this experience. Susie, a psychologist and astrologer, had been telling me for months that there was a need for a dramatic shift or change in my life. Eventually I met with a medical intuitive. A medical intuitive is able to perceive the underlying spiritual and psychological reasons for an illness. He was quite direct with me. He stated that I needed to leave my current job and that I also needed to leave Dallas–Fort Worth. The choice was mine to make—stay and face further illness and/or death or leave in order to regain my health and my life. I was frightened. My fear became anger. How dare he tell me this? What does he know? What *does* he know? Damn! I struggled with the decision. What about Ruth? What about the wise women group? What about my home of nine years and the nineteen years I had lived in Texas? And where would I go?

I agonized. How could I make such a major decision about uprooting my life based on what most people would consider to be unfounded advice? How could I explain it to my family and friends let alone anyone else? Yet I knew in my heart that I had to make this change; that I had to leave.

The wise women gathered for a celebration that we affectionately called The Last Supper. Ruth and I reminisced about our friendship, made a commitment to stay in touch and cried as we said goodbye. I chose to move to Santa Fe, New Mexico, a place that offered a scenic, healing environment for the next stage of my recovery. I sorted through my possessions. I put my house up for sale and left everything to the realtor and the movers.

The morning I was leaving, Kathleen came over with breakfast and helped me get everything in the car, including my two cats, Smokey and Tre. Kathleen waved goodbye as I pulled out of the driveway. As I turned on my cell phone, I found a voice message from Ruth wishing me a safe trip. I really wanted her making the trip with me.

As I headed west to Santa Fe, I watched nineteen years of my life in Texas fade away in my rearview mirror. Through my tears, I saw the road ahead leading me to the hope of renewal, healing and life. Leaving is *so* bittersweet.

DOUBLE FEATURE

Rebecca Dixon

Before my husband was my husband, we were young, dumb and chose to live in Laramie, Wyoming. What can I say? We thought it would be more romantic to live in a state that had more cows than people. It wasn't. Nine months into our hellish tour, we got married. The day we returned from our honeymoon we were greeted by an early-morning call from my mother. My pap test had come back abnormal.

I was given the choice to have my biopsy in Laramie or go to Dallas. Like that was a difficult choice. I had images of Laramie's finest large animal vet, Dr. Cletus the Slackjawed Yokel, saying, "Don't worry, Mrs. Dixon, we'll get you fixed right up. Clem! Bring me the Swiss Army knife and the branding iron." Does that biopsy come with snow tires, Doc? I caught the first flight to Dallas.

As soon as I got off the plane my mother whisked me off to her massage therapist. To my mother, there were few problems that pampering and luxury couldn't cure. Later that evening, she gave me a luxurious gift, a full-length fur coat. As we danced around the pool during the lunar eclipse, we were both distractedly laughing, unable to be scared about the biopsy. I told Mom, "I'm going to walk in tomorrow and tell the nurse, 'Thank you, but I brought my own coat that opens in the front.'"

The next morning I met the doctor. He looked like a Texas rancher. So much for my educated decision. After the biopsy he looked at me and said, "Becca, it's real important that nothing penetrate your vagina for the next eight weeks. Ya hear me? You've just had a delicate surgery and penetration could lead to infection. Do you understand? Penetration—bad, could lead to infection." It's okay, doctor, it's not like my husband and I spend Saturday nights sticking Volkswagons and watermelons in there.

I was at my parents' house alone when the biopsy results came. "You need to see me today?" I asked. "It's what? Cancer...Are you sure, I mean, aren't I too young? Okay. Thank you, Doctor." Why was I thanking him? He told me I probably couldn't have children but "medical technology has come so far." Great. Dr. Rancher just informed me the conception of my children would involve a lab and a staff.

I called Steve in Wyoming as soon as I hung up from the doctor. He told me he wished he could be there with me and he loved me ever so. He said since we were both adopted it was fine with him if we decided to carry on the family tradition of adoption. I never wanted to be pregnant more than at that moment. I later learned Steve called his best man, Brady, and cried to him for over an hour.

I numbly shuffled to my parents' room. I was no longer twenty-six but six and I needed the comfort of their bed. I was half watching *The Price is Right* when Dad called. I told him everything I knew in one frantic, crying breath. "Where's your mother?" he asked. I told him she should be back soon but I felt so all alone and scared; his response was, "Well, Bec, I've got to go, I was just on a lunch break...I gotta be back in court." He hung up.

Mom arrived. As she came into the room and saw me, I started to cry. I reached my arms to her like a toddler who needed comfort. She sat on the side of the bed and held me. "What is it, Baby?" she asked. I told her everything through my sobs, including how Dad hung up on me. "You probably scared him," she said. "He didn't even know what a cervix was before all of this." I told her about not being able to have kids. She put her arms around me and rocked me gently, in that way that only mothers can, my head fitting perfectly in the slope of her long neck. "Honey," she cooed, "if I could have a baby I wouldn't have you. And if you want a nice, white baby, we'll get you one." She then brushed my hair until I fell asleep.

November was my final appointment. Dr. Rancher scrunched his face up and said, "There is still a risk of infection. Would your husband wear a condom?" I replied, "Doc, we're newlyweds. If we have to oil up ourselves and perform a German clog dance we will." I excitedly jumped on the next plane out of Dallas. Only to be delayed in Denver.

All passengers were eventually sent to the "customer service representative"—a woman with a pinched face, wearing a crocheted vest with hearts on it, she had obviously had all of the joy sucked out of her life. I told her in simple terms that I *really* needed to get home. She replied through her pursed lips, "All I can do for you is give you some drink and dinner coupons." I wanted to reach across that desk, grab her by that stupid vest and scream, "Look lady, I'm a newlywed, I haven't had any sexual gratification in eight weeks, so unless you are planning on sticking your head between my legs and getting busy, I suggest you put me on a plane *right now!*"

When I finally did make it home, we stumbled our way into the bedroom fumbling with buttons, snaps and zippers. We made sounds I was sure were being taped by the Discovery Channel. I had no idea that I could orgasm through my eyelids. After the smoke alarm went off and the house was cantilevered on its foundation, I smiled at my husband. There is nothing like beating cancer with a good humping.

Six years later, I'm living in Santa Fe when my dad calls. He has to have a procedure. "Dad, at your age, a procedure could mean a heart transplant, please be specific." He told me he had melanoma.

His doctors wanted to see if it had spread to his lymph nodes. It had.

Each month after the procedure something else came up: brain tumors, spots on lungs, freckles on eyes and a mass on his rib. All of which were unrelated and benign. I told him to stop going to the doctor because they were only succeeding in finding things that do nothing but scare the crap out of us. Now, I'm scared. He's supposed to live until he's ninety. Everyone in his family lives until they're ninety. Okay, it's a lumpy-bumpy-check-your-prostate-every-year ninety; but it's ninety. That's not now. I think about when he's gone. Who will give me the best day of my life again?

I was in the second grade. I had a dentist appointment and Dad took me. I was supposed to go back to school, but Dad decided to take me to lunch. I thought lunch was the ultimate treat, until he asked me, "Would you like to go see a movie? How about that *Star Wars?*" What? Did I hear that right? Dad *never* took a day off. He even worked Christmas Eve. Was he asking me to skip school and go see the movie everyone was talking about? I had to play it cool. I closed my gaping mouth, shrugged my shoulders and casually attempted a "Sure." Did I sound too excited? Is he kidding, or did he say he wanted to take me today, now?

We went to the movie and Dad told me about when he was a kid and he would spend all day at the movies watching double features. After that day he started calling me "Chewie" after the character Chewbacca. Even now when he calls me that, he catches my eye with a smile at our shared secret day. Every time I'm home we see at least two movies together.

Now, I want desperately to see him. I want to go for a walk with him and talk politics. I want to sit in a darkened theater with him and watch a double feature. I want to watch him walk up and down a grocery store aisle shaking each purchase and humming off tune.

I want the phone to ring and hear him on the other end yelling, "Bec! It's Dad," in his booming Texas accent.

My mouth gets a coppery taste when I think of what he's going through. Then I get mad. I wish it could be a grown-up mad, but once again, I'm six years old talking with the schoolyard bully. "Don't think you will win this one, cancer. We have plans this summer. My dad is my superhero and he will beat you."

We have movies to see and you're not invited!

And that's the truth, no matter what happens.

My Dumb Disease

Ron Christman

"**M**Y DUMB DISEASE." The words leap out at me from a poster showing a sad-faced, gaunt, bald grade school-aged child. The poster is behind the restroom door at the Laughing Lizard Café in Jemez Springs. After a weekend of intense writing at a workshop for people with cancer, it is a real shot between the eyes. I feel so sad for the child, the parents and grandparents.

That same night I wake from a hard sleep feeling sexy. Great to feel sexy after having lost much of my libido as a result of surgery for prostate cancer and being on a testosterone-reducing hormone treatment. Should I wake Corine—my life, my love, my wife of forty-one years? But she is sleeping a deep, exhausted sleep. She has been burning her nervous energy by doing chores while waiting for knee replacement surgery to fix a broken knee that healed improperly.

But I have gotten ahead of my story. I am Ron Christman, sixty-four years old and almost ready for Medicare. Diagnosed with prostate cancer in 1992, I had surgery which eventually failed and then embarked on attempts at more natural and less invasive approaches to healing my cancer, but to no avail. I felt better from the revised diets and lifestyle changes but there was no change in my prognosis. I began hormone ablatement treatment in 1999 for one year. This treatment reduces the testosterone to essentially zero, which slows or even stops the prostate cancer. The treatment results were good and now I have been off treatment for a year but may have to start again as the cancer becomes worse. I do worry about going back on the hormone treatment because of the bad side effects. Plus there is always the possibility the treatment will not work. But overall there is much to be thankful for.

Originally I am from a small dusty town in South Dakota. Hot in the summer and cold in the winter. My family, which consisted of my parents and me, was poor but never destitute. My mother was in ill health most of her life. When we lived on a farm for a few years, she had to work very hard and had a nervous breakdown. She was supposed to clean, cook, watch me, milk ten cows, plus keep a garden and do other farm chores. Meanwhile my dad worked six long days in the fields and then had to do farm chores on Sunday. Once when Mother was sick, my uncle and aunt were visiting. Mother got worse and my dad and uncle had to take her to the hospital while my aunt stayed with me. I was terribly worried. When they got back, my dad said how terrible my mother looked by the time they had gotten her to the hospital. I was moping around and went out behind the house, where I started crying. Dad eventually found me and I told him that I wanted my mother. He said he missed her too and started crying with me.

One of the great joys of my young life was getting a bicycle. They had all cost too much but finally one became available for $40. I rushed home to tell my mother and then my dad when he came home from work. I saw him and mother look at each other and sort of sigh. Later he went alone to get the bike. When he came riding home on it I was so excited that I was doing cartwheels on the lawn. It was many years later that I found out that my parents had to buy the bike on the installment plan. Guess I never knew how really poor we were.

Let's fast-forward to my junior year in college. Thanks to good fortune at finding an after-school job and some help from my parents, I managed to scrape money together to go to college. Some friends and I are sitting on the steps of the Student Union. We are checking out the freshman girls. This is a college that had four times as many men as women and you had to move quickly. A girl from my home town came charging up and introduced us to her roommate Corine something or other. This girl from my home town was a real talker and we all worried a little when we saw her coming because it was hard to have a short conversation with her. Corine on the other hand seemed quiet, small and looked scared. She had brown hair and glasses and was wearing a white blouse and a straight skirt. Little did I realize that she would become the love of my life, my wife, the mother of my children, and the rock that would help me deal with cancer.

At a social dance, I asked Corine if I could take her back to the dorm after the dance. In this more innocent time this meant driving her back to the dorm and maybe kissing her good night, but there were also subtle moves that happened. If you remember cars with bench seats in the front you can follow me. I escorted Corine to the driver's side door and she got in there. The test was then to see how far she moved across the seat. If the girl moved as far as possible away on the seat, well, not much might happen. On the other hand, Corine told me years later that because she thought I was shy and needed encouragement, she sat close to me. So both having passed this test we got off to a fun start.

Now fast-forward to 1992. Corine suggests I get a PSA test. This test that helps detect if a man has prostate cancer. So I get the test and receive a real shock. My PSA reading is elevated, but nothing shows on the prostate biopsy. The test is repeated six months later and this time the PSA reading is even higher and the biopsy is positive. Oh rats. What a blast. Research, reading, decisions to make with inadequate data. Worry, worry. Finally decide on surgery. Goes well, results look good for a couple years and then the PSA starts creeping up again. Good grief, now what? After much agonizing, we decide to use a less invasive, natural approach involving physical, mental, emotional and spiritual changes to our lives. This is all nerve-wracking. What we call life-and-death decisions. My life or death! How could I have done any of this without Corine? She is my rock, my support group, always helping and supportive.

It could have been luck that caused me to marry Corine, but to me it seems more like it was ordained by a higher power. She happened to be rooming with a girl from my home town who introduces us. Much later we find out that my dad and her uncle and my aunt and her mother were childhood best friends, the families had adjacent farm homesteads, and even more surprising, our grandparents came from and knew each other in the same German/Russian town in South Russia.

In 1992 I was nearing the end of my career as a software engineer, originally at Sperry and most recently at the lab in Los Alamos. Typically I was a person who thought logically and believed that emotions should be controlled. As part of our alternative approach, Corine and I went to macrobiotic cooking training. I was hugely offended when the counselor we met with there suggested therapy as part of the plan. But with some not-so-gentle prodding from Corine and logical thinking on my part, I began going to therapy several times each month with my therapist, Irving. Part of the therapy has been learning how to think with the creative, non-logical side of my brain. Irving suggested I write poetry to get my emotions out, and while I resisted at first, I finally began trying even though I thought poetry was pretty dumb. This was an exercise in bad poetry, no pressure to make lines rhyme, no worries about flow, just get the emotions out. Bad stuff stored in your head has an impact on your physical health. Writing poetry was at first a big stretch for my technical brain but now it is a way of life. A part of me. Thanks, Irving.

My biggest fear is that I will get so sick that I will be completely dependent on other people. Having Corine, my children or a nursing home take care of me would be just awful. Having someone dress me, feed me, help me to the bathroom would be more than I could bear. Ring the call button and wait. Ring and wait. Ring and wait. The total loss of control, the endless days staring at the walls, no ability to leave. God, my stomach just knots up at the thought.

There have been many blessings in my life, including supportive friends, family and most important the support and love of Corine. A significant physical blessing is that I have been able to maintain a close to normal lifestyle in spite of the cancer. I have never had any symptoms from the cancer although I have had significant symptoms from some of the treatments. So we are able to do fun activities like dancing. Several years ago Corine dragged me to the Senior Center so we could learn to dance. This was a lot more complicated than we expected and I began to realize that I needed more help than I was getting in an informal setting. So I gave Corine and me six private dance lessons for her birthday. By the time that was over, I was hooked. So we continued, and since last year was our fortieth anniversary, we rented Fuller Lodge and gave ourselves a big anniversary party complete with a live band. Rather than do something stodgy like an informal anniversary waltz, we did chore-ographed dance solos of the rumba and tango.

After our anniversary party dance solos, I read this poem to Corine in front of the audience.

> *One of the big surprises of my life*
> *Is loving Corine more than I did*
> *When we got married.*
> *This woman in my life has become my life.*
> *My best friend, my dance partner,*
> *My ski partner, my biking partner*
> *Instead of only my lover.*
> *When we first got married,*
> *I had always thought that*
> *Young people had more fun.*

That old people married 40 years
Were just existing with a quiet love.
But love is not quiet at 40 years.
It is stronger than ever.
Our years of being together through
Good times and bad have tempered,
Strengthened and sharpened our love.

The fear of "My Dumb Disease" is always with me, but it does not stop me from enjoying life.

SURPRISES

Pelican Lee

My longtime friend Moon was dying of melanoma that summer I found lumps in my breast. She'd known she had melanoma for nine years, and had been doing alternative things for it. Like putting chewed-up grass on it, and later a cream she sent away to the Bahamas for. Her melanoma would shrink and then disappear, just to pop out again later right next to where it had been. She'd thought she had the melanoma under control, but now she was dying. Moon was dying at Arf, the women's community where she lived in the foothills of the Sangres. There was plenty of space for all of us to gather. In the evenings, we'd all go into her house and sing. Moon was the Song Queen, sometimes reminding us in whispers of the words to songs from years ago that we couldn't quite remember.

Like Moon, I prefer alternative healing methods, but now I was scared. I watched Moon shrivel up to skin and bones with a cancer that might not have killed her if it had been treated medically a long time ago. So I went for a mammogram. It showed three lumps in my breast, but everyone said that usually stuff on mammograms wasn't cancer. When I went to Doctor Cheryl, she told me that I would have to have a stereotactic needle biopsy because one of the lumps was underneath another. Instead of a regular surgical or needle biopsy, this method uses X-rays and computer technology. It was weeks until the appointment. But I didn't give it a lot of thought because my focus was on Moon. The morning of my appointment finally came, and I knew I wouldn't go, because Moon was so close to death I couldn't leave her. So I called and rescheduled. Moon died that night, and the next day thirty-five of us buried her at Arf.

Two weeks later, I went to Santa Fe Radiology for the biopsy with my beloved and supportive partner, Rebecca. Rebecca's father had also died the week before and we'd been to Iowa for his funeral. My "to do" list was longer than a horse's tail. We were bouncing from one death to another, overwhelmed with emotions. What was one more biopsy?

They wouldn't let Rebecca come into the room with me, and once I went in, I could see why. It was large enough only for the table I would lie on, and loads of equipment. Barely space enough for the technician and radiologist to move between the machines. I wasn't looking forward to this, especially without Rebecca to hold my hand and comfort me.

The technician had me lie face down on the high table, with the breast in question hanging down through a circular hole, clamped tight in a mammogram machine that was under the table. First they worked on the problematic deep lump near my chest wall. That lump was a half-inch deep, even squeezed between the plates. It took a lot of time to locate it and to line up the machine to get computerized coordinates. Then I was given a local anesthetic in my breast with a painful burning needle and the radiologist, in a flash appearance, cut a quarter-inch slit in my breast and shot a needle through the slit into the lump. I was not to move from the time the technician got the coordinates until the needle was shot in.

With each punch of the needle there was such a sudden pain, I couldn't help but jump with the stunning impact, and muffled an "oof!" into the pillows my head was wedged between. The plates held my breast so tightly that even with me jumping, my breast didn't move. They took five samples from that lump. Then they did the surface lumps, four samples from each one. It seemed to never end in that chilly, stuffy room, my body cramped in this awkward position, barely able to move. They told me what good endurance I have.

The sympathetic technician said I should get the results within forty-eight hours, and if not, to call her. The second day passed with no phone call. I wasn't allowing myself to get worried, but Rebecca wanted relief, and urged me to make phone calls. So I called the sweet technician, my ally. She'd make some calls, and if I heard nothing in twenty minutes, I was to call her back. A call came, and it was Doctor Jody, Cheryl was on vacation. He was terribly sorry to tell me that all three tumors were positive for cancer. My ears started ringing. I could barely breathe. This was not what I was expecting at all. What do I do now? I had no plan. I sat there at the phone, unable to move.

My insides were shaking. Rebecca came in and I blurted out to her that all three lumps were cancer, and then I saw the shock and concern on her face. Days later, when I finally saw Doctor Cheryl, I learned that with three tumors, there was no choice, I would have to have a mastectomy. If she'd taken out those three lumps, there wouldn't be much left anyway. I already felt scarred and damaged. I could feel the hardness from the biopsies under the three little bandages. My beautiful soft breast was already gone. I wasn't so upset about losing a breast, I was more afraid I would die. With three cancer tumors, what chance did I have? Rebecca was terribly afraid that she would lose me.

I watched the morning sunlight creep across the wall of the hospital room, waiting for Rebecca to come. Knowing her, she would've asked last night what time she was allowed to come, and would not appear one minute earlier. Sometimes I cursed her Quaker honesty. Someone had told us that the nurses allowed spouses to stay past visiting hours, so we planned that Rebecca would stay late last night.

When I had come out of surgery, I was comforted by the presence of my friends, and enjoyed listening to them laugh and carry on. I was still drugged and was drifting in and out of consciousness. Teresa doctored me for a long time with the white eagle feather. It danced over my bandages and my entire body, especially my arm, to protect it from lymphedema so that I'd be able to continue going into the sweat lodge. Heat from saunas, hot tubs or sweat lodges can cause lifelong problems with lymphedema, but the sweat lodge feeds my spirit and helps my healing. I had my lesbian family all around me—those here and those far away, sending cards, prayers and energy. Never before had I felt the healing touch of so many people's concerns and prayers and hopes, that carried me through cancer as if on wings. With their help, I flew.

The end of visiting hours came, and everyone left except Rebecca. She moved a chair closer to the head of the bed and I was happy to have some private time with her. She held my hand and I told her everything I could remember from when I hugged her goodbye before the cute gay nurse took me into the operating room. He was so obviously gay, I had to come out to him before they put me under. I wanted to hear how it had been for Rebecca in the waiting room, but just then, an aide came in and said that visiting hours were over. Rebecca told him that she was a spouse, could she stay a while longer? He said he would find out. So we carried on. It wasn't late, I wanted her to stay. Later the floor nurse came by and told Rebecca that she could stay a while longer.

Not much later, I couldn't believe what I was seeing when two uniformed officers suddenly appeared at the foot of my bed. I was so startled, I jumped, and the little brown stuffed bear in my arm jumped, and the officer jumped, saying, "What's that?" Little Bear has fooled cats—the cat slinking on her belly with ears back trying to get close enough to sniff Little Bear as we tried not to howl with laughter. The officer said that they'd come to escort Rebecca out of the hospital. Rebecca was totally calm, just got up and went out with them with barely a goodbye to me. I was left alone in the room, numb from the drugs, wondering if this was a dream or what? Before long, the aide came by. He knew that we'd been given mixed messages, tried to explain about a turf war between the nurses. He stayed for quite a while, telling me a long story about a cousin that I couldn't follow at all, but I appreciated his kindness.

Later Rebecca told me that the guards were embarrassed, thought they had been sent to take out a drunk. Instead, they found this lovely serene silver-haired Quaker. Once she got into our truck to go home, she yelled out her frustration without jeopardizing the care I would get.

Perhaps that charge nurse didn't like the noisy bevy of lesbians in my room. She didn't recognize that Rebecca *was* my spouse, that we'd gotten married five years before in the Quaker Meeting and that we both wear wedding rings.

When my cancer anniversaries come, I celebrate one fewer year to go on Tamoxifen. I sure do hate that stuff. Five years on a drug. Before this, the only drugs I ever took were illegal. Tamoxifen put me into menopause in a big way. The hot flashes are the worst part. Or more like, never knowing how hot or cold the room is because my body is on its own thermostat, which never stays in one place. Either I'm burning up and sweating, or I'm shivering with chills. No one warned me about those chills, when I wrap up in everything I can get a hold of, and am still freezing. So now my wardrobe has been reduced to shirts that button, so I can get them off and on quickly and I only button a few buttons—what's the point of buttoning more? More than once I've been embarrassed to find myself out in public with a half-buttoned shirt.

I'll never forget the first really intense hot flash. I didn't know what was happening to me. I'd walked to the neighborhood Furr's for a few groceries and was standing in the checkout line, my hands full with the green chile and cheese and chips when it hit. I suddenly felt so hot and nauseous, I wondered if I was going to faint. Oh God, not here, they'd call an ambulance, it would be a disaster. I was sweating so much under my down jacket and wool hat, I could feel sweat trickling down my front. I hung onto the checkout counter, gulped air, and hoped no one noticed. Somehow I managed to get through the line and pay my money. I slowly walked outside and sat down on the sidewalk with my back against a wall, and sat there, wondering if people going into Furr's thought I was homeless or something, until I felt strong enough to walk home. Only later did I figure out that it had been just a powerful hot flash.

Today I worry that I've forgotten the lessons and gifts of cancer, and have grown complacent and sunk back into my before-cancer life of waiting for future fulfillment instead of living in the moment. Like I thought my life would start when I finally found the perfect partner, but now I've been with the perfect (well, mostly!) partner for twelve years, and I'm still waiting for my life to begin. Still plowing through that never-finished "to do" list. If I ever get through that list and have nothing more to add, will my life begin or will it be over?

A MOTHER'S STORY

LouAnn Asbury

I can still hear the wailing and feel the terror...my wailing, my terror. She had said, "Mom, I think I have cancer." How could that be? My daughter Holli, only twenty-nine years old, just married a few weeks before. How could she have cancer? There was no cancer on my side of the family or her father's side. It wasn't possible. It had to be a mistake. The lab must have gotten her biopsy tissue confused with another patient's.

But she had said that the doctor double-checked, repeating the biopsies because he couldn't believe the results. Actually the pap had not been normal during her annual routine exam two weeks before the wedding, but the gynecologist had decided to wait until after Holli's wedding to do more testing, thinking that waiting three weeks would not be harmful. He didn't want to spoil her plans for her dream wedding. Now he was sure there was a malignancy in her cervix. He said she needed to see him in the office the next morning and he would explain.

"I'll be on the next flight to Dallas," I told her. "I'll stay with you as long as you want me to."

"But Mom, how can you leave your church? Who will preach for you?"

I told her that was no problem. I told her they could carry on without me and that I would be there early in the morning in time for her appointment. I hung up, then made flight reservations and called the necessary people to take over, saying, "I don't know when I'll be back." They said, "Don't worry about us; just take care of Holli." They said they would be praying.

In the 100-year-old Methodist church in rural Louisiana, the word spread quickly.

Holli and John met me at the Dallas–Forth Worth Airport, and we drove straight to her gynecologist's office in Arlington. As the three of us sat in front of his desk, he drew a picture…a picture of Holli's cervix and uterus with three tumors. Not one, but *three*. Pathology indicated they were all malignant. He had made an appointment for her with an oncological gynecological surgeon in Forth Worth, and that surgeon would see us as soon as we could get there. An hour later I was holding Holli's hand as she lay on the exam table.

"It hurts, Mom," she said. "I'm still sore from the biopsy."

The surgeon apologized. "I'm sorry. I know this is painful." I liked the sound of his soft, gentle voice. If Holli had to have this horrible surgery, I trusted him to do it.

The surgeon said he thought the tumors were contained, but he would need to do a radical hysterectomy to check all the lymph nodes. With his gloved hand, he traced a line on Holli's abdomen to show her how large the incision would be. He would need a lot of room to look around. She would have a scar that stretched from one hip bone to the other. From my own experience I knew how painful that would be and how long it would take for Holli's abdomen to feel "normal" again. Surgery was scheduled for two days later.

Holli was a second-grade teacher, and she decided to teach her class the next day before letting a substitute teacher take over. I went with her and remembered my own days as a second grade teacher. Holli was much more gifted, much more creative than I had been. It was perfectly clear how much she loved each child, and how much they adored her. I didn't know that I could feel such pride. Tears welled up in my throat as I realized that Holli would never be able to give birth to her own child. She had waited to marry John until she was ready to have children. And now it was too late. My heart was breaking, breaking wide open as I took in all that cancer could mean.

I was on automatic pilot on the way to the hospital the next morning. I didn't dare feel all that was going on inside of me. I had to be available for Holli and John and I knew I would have to deal with my own grief and sense of tragedy later. John was a basket case. His mother had died of cancer and he thought cancer meant death. I would need to take care of him for the next hours during surgery. He had never been through anything like this...and this was his bride whom he worshipped.

I kissed Holli as she was wheeled into surgery, and then the wait began. Sitting in the waiting room with Holli's father and his new wife...how awkward that was. How I resented what he had done, suddenly leaving me after fifteen years of marriage with no warning, breaking up our family. He had said he would not sue for child custody if I allowed our fourteen-year-old son David to live with him, and he would "allow" twelve-year-old Holli to stay with me. And so Holli and I had suffered together as we started a new life following the turmoil of divorce. We had always been very close, the kind of relationship I had longed to have with my mother, but the breaking up of our family brought us even closer. As an adult, Holli had always said I was her best friend.

And now, six years after Holli was diagnosed, I am waiting again. Waiting for Holli to adopt my grandchild. Is this waiting anything like sitting in the waiting room during those long, endless hours of Holli's surgery? Back then I was waiting for the moment when the surgeon said, "She's fine. The lymph nodes are clean. She's in a lot of pain; it'll be a long recovery—about two months." "She's fine," he said. And I heard, "She'll live cancer-free. All the cancer has been cut out of her body. No more worries. She's fine." That's what I heard—that's what I wanted to hear, needed to hear.

And ever since that moment six years ago, I think I believe Holli is fine...there is no more cancer...the cancer is gone from her body. I can't even imagine how I would feel if her cancer comes back. I don't want to think about that. I want to think about going to China with Holli to pick up her baby girl—my baby granddaughter. I want to think about seeing Holli and her baby, holding the baby, loving the baby.

For five years now Holli has been talking about adopting a baby girl from China. She left John two years ago. John didn't want to adopt a baby, did not want to have a baby that was not his blood. I have wondered why she keeps waiting to start that adoption process. Is it because she still wants to give birth, and can't bring herself to accept the reality of her loss? But Holli is making a life for herself. She has created a unique career teaching elementary teachers how to teach math in creative ways. Other teachers watch her teach their students, learning how she does it. She's buying a house now, a house with a room for a nursery and a backyard with big, old oak trees. The house comes with a swing set already in place under the shade of the trees. She's moving into her new life with hope and expectation. And that life, as I see it, has no room for cancer.

THE CONTRIBUTORS

Deborah Milton Spaulding

CANCER AND OTHER TRAVELS

Christine Barber

WORDS

Lisa Avedon

A PASSENGER

Sylvia Vizcaya Alderson

STRAWBERRIES

Mary Tufft

THE DEEPEST SURRENDER

Michael Burt

KATHLEEN AND A NECTARINE,
BOTH IN THE IMAGE OF GOD

Lena Albert

BREATHE

Pamela Avis

SISTERS, FACE TO FACE

Jennie Reasoner-Wagner

In the Beginning

Janet Greene, M.D.

A DOCTOR'S JOURNEY

Willow Rose

SWIMMING TO THE SURFACE

Dedre Umoja Will

THE OTHER PATIENT

Deborah Gunderman

LEAVING

Rebecca Dixon

DOUBLE FEATURE

Ron Christman

MY DUMB DISEASE

Pelican Lee

SURPRISES

LouAnn Asbury

A MOTHER'S STORY

Patsy Sears

FLOATING IN THE RIVER

Linda Braun

An Impressive Growth

David DeVary

IT'S A FAMILY THING

Lora Morton DeVary

LIVING WITH SOMEONE ELSE'S CANCER

Alice Kitselman

WAITING TO GET A LIFE

Eleanor Castro

I CALL IT MY CANCER

Judi Jaquez

CAN A WOMAN WITH ONE BREAST
AND NO HAIR BE SEXY?

MaryAna Eames

LEARNING HOW TO ASK,
REMEMBERING HOW TO CRY

Barbara Ness

MOVING ON

Argos MacCallum

CROSSROADS

Judy Kiphart

2 A.M.

Nancy Henry

THE TIME OF MY LIFE

Blythe Jane Richfield

I WISH I'D NOTICED
THAT MY BODY WAS A TEMPLE

FLOATING IN THE RIVER

Patsy Sears

I remember the day when I first realized something was wrong. I was taking a bath, and I noticed that one side of my abdomen was bigger than the other. I was definitely lopsided. Suddenly, all my denial of bothersome little symptoms fell away, and I knew that I had cancer. I began to shake and cry in a full-flung anxiety attack. My husband held me and calmed me, but I knew in my heart that something was terribly wrong.

The next morning I went to get a sonogram on my gall bladder because I'd been experiencing a lot of heartburn. The tech finished surveying my liver and gall bladder without finding anything abnormal. "Look over on the left side," I suggested. "It's been feeling a little hard there." The tech took a look as I had asked, and I saw her face pale. Wordlessly, she ran out of the room to call her supervisor. From that moment on, nothing was ever the same again. I felt like I had fallen into a cold river, caught inexorably in the current, unable to swim to safety. I saw familiar landmarks pass on the shore as I floated farther and farther downstream. I didn't drown. But now I'm in another country where I don't recognize the landscape, and I'm not sure how much farther I can swim.

I don't remember going to sleep at the hospital. I remember the anesthesiologist introducing herself, a pretty young woman with dark ringlets. Then I don't remember any more. Sometimes I imagine what the two surgeons must have said while I was out. "Gosh, what a mess!" "Egads! This thing is huge!" That was before my next surgery when I got smart and told them what to say. Only kind things! Only positive healing statements!

I really don't remember, but when I woke up everything hurt and nothing worked right. I wonder if those doctors left some foreign object inside me that disrupted my center of gravity, my polarity, so now I can't tell which way I'm going or which way is up. I feel like a compass needle, spinning out of control, that can't find its way to north.

As I float along on my back, sometimes I see a familiar object on the shore. See there! It's a tail wagging. It's a dog! It's Augie the Doggie, more formally known as St. Augustine of Hippo, because as a puppy he resembled nothing more than a fat little hippo. Augie is also a saint. My youngest grandchild can explore his ears and eyes with a sharp baby finger, and Augie will not move—and never growls. He endures it all with a placid peace that only a saint could cultivate.

Augie makes me laugh. That's worth a lot when you have cancer. He taints any room he's in with his own aroma. He ambles toward me duck-footed with his ears laid back sheepishly, and his beautiful wolf-like muzzle in a shit-eating grin. He doesn't lick me, but he nudges. God protect me from Augie's nudges, especially if I have a cup of tea in my hand. St. Augie, he truly is. I love him best of all. He is my amiable, natural, fur-coated self, who explodes with a burst of barking when the deer dare to invade our yard. In my dreams, I run with Augie after the deer, our tails waving wildly in the wind.

Floating in that cold river, I pretend I'm on a float trip. I used to worship the sun with my body. Lying on my back with my eyes closed, carried gently on the current, I found an oblivion known nowhere else in my life. The yellow sun oozing through my closed eyelids transported me to desert islands, and palm trees, and visions of new life. Sun-yellow has always meant full-speed-ahead to me. Be happy! Love life! Live!

Twenty-one-month old Jonah loves yellow. He's young to have a favorite color, but he's also very determined. He calls himself "yellow boy," and he carries around the yellow markers from my game of Sorry clenched tightly in his tiny fist. I've designed an afghan for him. He's chosen the colors himself—yellow and purple, and maybe a little bit of red, but mostly yellow. I wonder if it's genetic—his and my love of yellow. It seems to go with what I call our "up gene," the one that makes me teeter on a rock above the river, the one that compels Jonah, small as he is, to climb to the top of the couch via the end table, or to stand at the top of the slide with his arms held out like an airplane.

I'm knitting that blanket for Jonah, stitch by stitch, knitting my love for him, my love for life, for the color yellow. I'm knitting into every stitch a prayer—that I will survive, that Jonah will survive: his climbs, his falls, his attempts to reach the "up" in life, to climb to the sky, to reach the color yellow.

Christmas was pretty hard this year. Two days before Christmas, I found a new lump. I tried valiantly not to tell my family until Christmas was over. I didn't want to ruin their Christmas, but I felt like such a liar every time I answered their question, "How are you?" with "Fine. Just fine."

Christmas dinner barely happened. Oh, the chicken got stuffed and baked, but there wasn't much to go with it. No one felt like cooking, even less like eating. We lit the candles and opened the Bible to read the familiar story. But it was just words. As the night darkened, in desperation, I suggested going outside to see the candles through the window, hoping to see a framed tableau of hope. We opened the door and stepped out on the deck with the dogs at our side. Suddenly, the thick quiet was split with the most horrendous wailing and caterwauling. Four jaws, human and canine, literally fell open. What strange angelic choir was this come to declare

Christmas? Coyotes over the hill, singing, "Peace on earth, good will to all who suffer."

I'm sick of hearing that cancer is transformational. I liked my life just fine before. It didn't need to be transformed. I was progressing on my journey *just fine*!

And then whammo! Cancer! It doesn't feel so much like transformation as like being blown to pieces, to smithereens, with body fragments careening into the sky like deadly little missiles and plunging back into the earth like meteor shards. And now I get to put the pieces back together, but I swear they're not all part of the same puzzle. Instead I have a shred of cloud-filled sky next to a piece of running water above a twisted remnant of a dog's tail below a lizard's splintered eye.

How do I put together these pieces I've been given—three surgeries, a poor prognosis, early retirement, treatments that leave me sick and breathless and in pain, sympathetic friends, grieving family, and a husband who can continue to function only when he denies the reality of my situation—how can I make these pieces into a coherent picture?

Transformation, schmansformation! I just want my life back. I'd be happy to trade all this deep life-and-death talk for one sweet illusory moment of life before cancer—before cancer stripped me naked and flung me in this cold river. And now I'm just floating, and I'm terribly tired, and I don't know how much farther I can swim.

AN IMPRESSIVE GROWTH

Linda Braun

In February of 1954 I was the first child born to Irene and David. Thank heavens I was a girl—had I been a boy they would have named me Lance, a name I generally associate with the piercing of boils.

My parents were fond of Dr. Spock—not the one with the funny ears—the one who claimed to know everything about raising children. I loved the colorful birds that hung over my crib, but I didn't like spending long dark nights alone there. I cried and screamed and cried and screamed trying to let my parents know this wasn't OK, but Dr. Spock said, "Don't spoil your child, let them cry it out." Left to my own devices I rocked back and forth and banged my head on the white wooden headboard. It was a strange mode of comforting myself, but by golly I was expressing my power—every night the rocking and banging rolled my crib clear across my room. I'll show you, Dr. Spock!

I'm two years old and I've learned the word "no." I'm fascinated by my mother's reaction every time I say it. Secretly thrilled that it drives her crazy, I use it a lot and the battle is on.

At four I love the chocolatey milk that Bosco syrup induces and I only eat sandwiches of American cheese on Wonderbread with the crust cut off.

I fell in love when I was eight—with Jerry Mathers, the Beaver. I watched religiously every day, inspired by his antics and bowled over by his freckled cuteness. I wrote him copious letters and labored over drawings so they'd be good enough to send. Much to

99

my amazement, Jerry wrote back. He answered my questions, told me about his life and asked me about mine. He included a photo of himself which he signed "Love, your friend, Jerry Mathers, the Beaver."

As a teenager I was introduced to fashion magazines. I plummeted into a sea of despair—how would I ever look like that? And if I didn't, who would ever love me? My skinniness was in style, but my oh-so-curly hair was not. Determined to straighten it I wrapped it around my head, rolled it on a coffee can, and covered it with metal hairclips. I spent a lot of time under a huge beehive of a hairdryer, praying for success and low humidity.

At twenty I had made it through my second year of college and my mother and I had started to build a kinder, friendlier relationship. Back home for the summer I was off to visit a friend in Pennsylvania for the weekend. I hollered "Bye, Mom," kissed her on the cheek and was off. Two hours of train travel later, my friend opened the door and said, "Your mother had a heart attack, she's in intensive care." I was stunned. By the time I got back home visiting hours were over. My father assured me she was resting comfortably and that the doctors thought she would be OK. I cried my eyes out all night long, hating myself for all the lying, fighting and deliberate rebellion I had manufactured over the years. I curled up tightly on my side trying to escape the unbearable ache in my belly. I couldn't conceive of life without my mother. Around 5 a.m. the phone rang, and seconds later my father let out a moan whose tone and pitch I will never forget. My mother was dead. A massive heart attack at age forty-four.

I returned to New York City, frozen in my pain and loneliness. My closest companion was Lucy, a calico cat I adopted from the shelter. Through the practice of yoga I began to unfold and started making eye contact again. I completed my twenties and began my thirties. I was dating, I was an artist—but I longed for nature and her wide open spaces.

When I closed my eyes I saw the snow-capped mountains of northern New Mexico. I rubbed my eyes to dispel this silliness. But they kept coming back. "Santa Fe," I mutter, and purchase a plane ticket to get me there. Just before I leave, my grandmother calls. "Listen Linda dear, my friend Florrie's son, Len, lives in Santa Fe, he's a very nice Jewish man, here, I'll give you his phone number."

My visit to this City of Faith was stellar. I found my way around without the slightest idea of where I was going. I hardly slept but felt clear as a bell—something else was guiding me here. I met Len at his custom tile factory. He's friendly, we chat and he gives me a tour. When he goes off to answer the phone I wander around by myself. "Can I help you?" asks a man unloading tiles from cylindrical kilns. Our eyes meet and the attraction is huge. "Whoa, girl," I say to myself as our conversation ignites. I panic for a moment when I hear his name—Gershon—oh, please don't be part of some strange cult, I fervently pray. When Len reappears he offers me a job. "I'll take it," I reply with a giant smile on my face.

Gershon and I were married in less than a year and I was happier than I ever thought possible.

Approaching forty I kept waking up with this strange swelling above my left eye and I was having excruciating headaches. I went for a neurological checkup.

"You seem fine to me," said the doctor, "but let's get a CAT scan, just to be sure." Post-scan, arriving home I had barely begun to tell Gershon about my afternoon when the phone rang. It was the neurologist. "You have an impressive growth," he said. "What? What's that?" we asked. "It's a very large tumor in the left temporal lobe of your brain. It needs to be removed immediately."

That was seven years and four surgeries ago. For the first surgery they shaved the left side of my head and made a large horseshoe-shaped incision. They peeled back the skin and cut out a big chunk of my skull. They moved my brain over, excised the golf ball–sized tumor and stapled me back together.

In the second surgery, they went in through my skull again, moved my brain over and cut a window through my sphenoid wing bone, so they could go down into my left orbit. This beast of a tumor had wrapped itself around my optic nerve, filled the back of my orbit and ventured dangerously close to my cavernous sinus. Three surgeons labored for nine hours in my head. They got most but not all of it out, so I followed up with thirty-five days of radiation.

For the third surgery they went into my orbit through the bone on the side, and I walked out of the hospital the following day.

Surgery number four, which by the way happened on this same date —April 21—just last year, was by far the easiest. They simply made an incision in the crease of my eyelid and pulled the sucker out.

And I don't even have cancer! I have recurrent atypical sphenoid wing meningioma. Can you say that? It's technically benign, but according to statistics I'm due for more recurrences.

Don't get me wrong—I consider myself to be very, very lucky. When I awoke from the first surgery I was amazed to find myself singing praises to God I never knew I had in me. Since then God also hears my outrage, despair, fears and demands. We have a well-rounded relationship.

On my good days I know that no matter how I am cut into or rearranged, the real me can never be touched or diminished. The tumors, and all they've brought up, have been gifts. But now I'm beginning to understand that it is my whole life—every moment of this human experience—that is the gift, the ultimate gift.

P.S. It's late at night, in the midst of the Cancer Monologue workshop, and I have just completed my piece. Exhausted and exhilarated I lie down in bed and place my hand on my chest. "Hmmm, what's this?" I think, feeling a small, hard lump under my finger. It wasn't the center of my breastbone as I had hoped. It was a pea-sized lump that didn't hurt and moved freely under my skin, just like a benign fibroid I'd had years ago. An excisional biopsy two days later revealed that this was an aggressive lump of breast cancer. I was devastated, certain that death was soon to follow. All along I'd assumed that at least my meningiomas granted me karmic immunity from the horrors of cancer. No such luck; I spent the summer doing chemo and the fall doing radiation. And now, one year later, I am happy to report that I feel great and am still completely alive!

It's a Family Thing

David DeVary

Most of my family life has revolved around cancer. Most everyone in my family has died from it. My parents, grandparents, brother—everyone except my youngest brother. He has AIDS. Oh…and my son, Davy, he was in his early thirties when he died of a drug overdose, not cancer. You can probably see why I might have a problem or two with cancer…and death. In addition, why I'd have a few isolation and abandonment issues, to say nothing of the great need to have some control in my life.

To say I needed a few screws tightened…well, for instance: Some years ago, my shrink had a hell of a time convincing me of how insane I was to believe that as long as I kept smoking I'd be safe from cancer. My response? "Just look, none of them smoked and look what happened to them."

The losses, the losses, they were so great. The horror, how can a four-year-old go on without his Bobo, his railroad engineer, next-door grandpa. My Bobo would take me everywhere with him. I don't think I ever felt more loved. We'd fish for hours, play catch, look for four-leaf clovers and tell each other stories. Since he couldn't read or write, Bobo relied on storytelling. Being totally colorblind, you can only imagine what his side of my coloring book looked like, magical. As magical as those long weekend fishing trips were. Bobo and all of that disappeared with liver cancer when I was only four.

Not more than a year later, my grandma died of skin cancer. It was an ugly, smelly skin cancer. A great loss for me, especially, because she was the only one who could protect me from my crazy mother. I was in deep shit!

Mom was easy to love and hate. She was beautiful, both my daughters look like her, wonderfully outgoing and oh...so self-centered. A clotheshorse who loved to entertain, which posed a great problem in our family. Dad made very little money. The humiliating arguments Mom had with Dad over dinner sure put a damper on mealtime. I was fourteen, she a mere forty-two when she lost her heroic fight with breast cancer. What a battle it was. I remember near the end, Mom was eating lot of unflavored gelatin. One of her doctors explained that gelatin is a pure protein and the cancer would feed on that instead of on her. That made me sick!

Five generations of women in her family had all died from breast cancer by the time they were forty. From the time I was about ten, I remember Mom, Dad, and my two younger brothers being so afraid of cancer and of her dying. What were we to do? Denny, the baby, was only three or four at the time. There wasn't anything that they wouldn't try, from throwing out all our aluminum pots and pans to having hundreds of prayers and masses said. It all came to a very sad and painful end that left Dad a broken man and did some major damage to the rest of us. We were a pretty sorry lot. Although I had a job at my uncle's grocery store, I took on the running of the house and taking care of the younger kids. It was a lot of responsibility. In looking back, the whole ordeal both strengthened and weakened me. It really was too much for me at my age and put some dings in my physical armor.

However, the crack really started creeping down the middle of my forehead at the age of twenty-six. I guess I was not as strong as I thought. Mike, my twenty-four-year-old brother, was going down fast with testicular cancer. Up until this time, we had been talking about going into business together. Me the graphics man, Mike the printer.

That loss was finally too much. I became bulimic and nuts. Apparently, bulimia from the loss of a loved one is a pretty com-

mon reaction. However, being in advertising at the time, hardly anyone even noticed. Just one more nutcase in the creative department.
To this day I still fight bulimia on and off.

Time went on and my life was pretty normal. However, in the middle of moving to Santa Fe in 1989, I lost my dad. My wife, new baby
daughter and I were still in Chicago when I got the phone call from
my stepmom that Dad was dying. I was alone in the car, speeding
down 66, and I started crying, realizing Dad had just died. I looked
at the clock. It was nine-fifteen a.m. When I arrived at the hospital
in Bloomington, Illinois, an hour and a half later, I need not have
asked. I was told he passed peacefully at nine-fifteen.

With the help of a little maturity, a lot of hard time on a shrink's
couch, and finally forgiving God by going back to the church, I han-
dled Dad's death much better. We had buried the hatchet some
years earlier and were able to be with each other. Dad had hardly
any ability to hide his feelings. A true "straight-shootin' son-of-a-
gun" if you ever saw one. A simple, sweet, rough man who never
had any idea of his incredible worth. Dad's values, morals and
incomparable inability to lie are his priceless gifts to me. Thankfully,
he never knew what the autopsy would reveal, that he also had cancer. A stroke took him before he had to suffer through the progres-
sion, treatments and trauma of his most dreaded illness.

About four years ago the fun really began when the urologist said
as soon as he looked at me, "I was right; it was more than an infection. Go get a CAT scan tomorrow." Two days later I was minus my
tumor-laden left testicle. In addition, since we found it so early,
instead of the suggested radical surgery, just a few extra hits of
chemotherapy should do it. Chemo sucks!

I've never been so sick in my life. My stomach violently reacted to
the drugs. So much so, the oncologist told me he was sure I was

going to bring in a gun and blow all their heads off. I told him it had crossed my mind.

I also had good days. One of my best days was at the local supermarket. I was literally starving because of chemo. Either not wanting to eat, or not being able to keep anything down. I was desperate, prowling the supermarket like a starving cat. Suddenly I saw it glowing. A lovely, smooth sweet potato!

Now there's a food with history, good history. Sweet potatoes are Christmas and Thanksgiving food. Something my whole family got together and shared. My God, I hardly have any family left. I still remember Grandma's sweet potatoes with lots of brown sugar and butter, a little cinnamon and nutmeg, toasted pecans and marshmallows on top. No way in hell will I ever be able to eat that! But maybe a simple baked one, maybe.

I was not disappointed, baked and mashed with a little salt and butter. It was heaven! Smooth, rich, sweet, and I kept it down. Yeah! It was the best day I'd had in a long time. Finally, something to eat.

But it was not to be. The second mouthful the next night was vile. The smell was even worse. I still have trouble with the smell today. But I will never forget how wonderful it was for that one day.

Then there was that other horrible unforgettable day. Oh God...Davy, my baby, my beautiful man up and die on me?! What's a daddy to do? The sadness, the grief...My God...I love you so much. I love you more than me. Relationships may come and go, but my son...I have no say; I just get to love you no matter what.

I realized today that you and Bobo were, with few exceptions, the only two guys who really knew who I was and loved me anyway. O my God! What am I going to do without you? I miss you so much; you were such a pain in the ass. You were forever pushing me to the edge, as you pushed yourself. You made me become more of a man than I thought I could. You made me into a father. Your father.

I had to love, care and guide you. You felt things so extremely. You were such a handful. On the other hand, you were such a sweet, sensitive macho-man. You were what I wanted to be: a handsome, macho hockey goalie. All those well-earned scars on that face. What a face it was! That killer smile made possible by an ill-caught hockey puck. Your two front teeth replaced with those beautiful, perfect white caps.

Even as a baby, you seemed so at home in your body. You were a natural athlete. Add to that, those eyelashes, so ridiculously long that we had to cut them when you were little. Most mornings, you could not get your eyes open because the sleepers gummed them up so. You fearless, accident-prone little shit! Evanston Hospital's ER knew us on a first-name basis, always there patching up one part of your body or another.

Oh God, my beautiful boy. The bipolar diagnosis was much too late. You had been self-medicating far too long. The torment you suffered was hell for both of us. Daddy couldn't make it go away as I could with the bad dreams. I so long to see you, 'cause Daddy could really use one of your smiles right about now. My brave warrior!

Having hardly any other choices, I have slowly learned how to deal with cancer and death the best I could. By allowing myself to feel, some of the exquisite heartbreaks seem to be in direct proportion to my ability to feel love more deeply. In practice, some days are a hell of a lot better than others. Nonetheless, the process is a noble and worthy pursuit.

My wife and my two incredible daughters love me. My baby brother loves me. My friends love me. But the most fun is being loved by my five grandbabies. I am grateful to be here today and constantly have to remind myself not to take it for granted, because today is a good day to be alive.

Living With Someone Else's Cancer

Lora Morton DeVary

It Was in the Prenup

Y ou don't marry someone who has lots of cancer in his family without at least an inkling that you may have to face the disease in your spouse (unless you're that much in denial). Still, the timing of David's disease came as a surprise. He was only in his fifties and looked very healthy (because he sits in the sun, risking skin cancer, but that's another issue). A pain in his groin, noticeable when we rode our horses, led to an ultrasound that revealed a tumor and a diagnosis of a testicular cancer common to guys in their late teens. He didn't tell me much about it, though. He explained more of the details to one of our riding buddies and I had to eavesdrop to learn what was going to happen.

On February 9, 1998, at three o'clock, David had surgery for "testicular masses." The "masses" were tested, and the doctor called him with those results two days later. "Oh, yikes," I heard David say softly while I was in the next room folding laundry. Even though we both normally use much stronger language than "yikes," I knew from his tone of voice that the news was neither good nor benign. We were looking at four rounds of chemo, one week on, three weeks off. I say "we" were looking at this thing because if you have a partner, the partner goes through the experience as well, in his or her own way. David did not seem too disturbed by the news but I admit that I was scared—not necessarily that he would die (his prognosis was excellent) but that there was so much of the unknown ahead of us.

The first person for me to tell, aside from my daughter, was my mother, who is very fond of David. He is her only son-in-law, balancing out the five daughters-in-law. I called her several times that day to tell her, but her phone wasn't working properly, so finally late in the afternoon, I called my older brother who lives near her and asked if by any chance he would see Mom soon. "As a matter of fact, she's coming to dinner tonight. Did you want me to pass along a message?"

I started crying. I told him that David had cancer. Then he started crying. "I'll tell her," he said, "but you're gonna owe me big time."

TOO MUCH OF A GOOD THING

Another aspect of the timing was that my father had died when I was ten, of a heart attack. When David was diagnosed, our daughter was also ten. I glanced up at God and questioned whether He was carrying His sense of irony a tad too far. Surely He wouldn't do that to her, to us. I knew my daughter was much closer to her dad than I had been to my father, and she would probably be much healthier if, in fact, she ended up losing her dad soon. But that didn't make it any more acceptable.

I love irony, but sometimes it can be obnoxious.

WAITING TO INHALE, TOO

From the very beginning, I felt that I had to be in charge of the household, the family and any business, not to mention David's health. I was terrified of screwing up because for the next few months I would have no backup, at least none who was in good health. It felt like an immense responsibility. My mother had become a widow when she was forty-two, raising six children by herself. When David was diagnosed, I was forty-eight, almost forty-nine, with one child. Still, I was overwhelmed.

David started chemo on March 30, 1998. About a month later, I met a friend for tea and told her what was happening. She remarked that I was handling it well. I said, what other choice is there? Afterward I thought about that for a while. I guess you could be frantic and loony, but you'd embarrass yourself and be no help to anyone, so why would you do that?

One way to cope is to avoid taking a deep breath. I felt that if I didn't disturb the molecules around me I wouldn't create anything negative. Taking a deep breath might imply a confidence I didn't have, and I was not about to tempt fate in any way.

This was my journal entry for April 22: In today's *Daily Word* [an inspirational booklet], it said, "When you come to the end of your rope, tie a knot and hang on."

THE TRADITIONAL GIFT IS A BARF BAG, ISN'T IT?

During the stretch of chemo, our 20th wedding anniversary arrived in the middle of an "on chemo" week. I knew that David didn't feel well, but darn it, we had been together for twenty years and that was worth celebrating. I didn't want to be cruel, but I really needed to reward myself with a dinner out that night, and I told him that he could stay home or come with me and our daughter. He dragged himself to my favorite restaurant where we were given a booth, and he sat with his back at the end of it and his legs stretched out on the seat. He ordered an appetizer at which he picked a bit. I ordered my favorite entree and enjoyed it, and we had crème brûlée for dessert.

Days later, David told me he didn't remember a thing about the evening.

SIDE EFFECTS

These are some of the side effects of chemo that we'd been told about: Dave's fingertips might become a little numb. He'd probably lose his hair, he may have nausea. The truth: all that and more. We were also advised to postpone a trip to Europe we'd been planning, as he would be susceptible to infection and who knows what he'd be exposed to. Boo.

This is one of the effects of chemo that they didn't tell us about: David lost some of his hearing, the higher notes, as in a woman's voice. Selective loss, a wife might ask? No, a hearing test confirmed the condition. It seems that one of the chemicals in David's chemo mix was able to flatten the hairs in the inner ear that pick up higher sounds, preventing the transmission of those vibrations. He was told that this was irreversible, but not bad enough—yet—to warrant a hearing aid. How this affects me personally is that I have to repeat myself an awful lot, and face him if I want to improve the odds of his understanding what I'm saying. It also means that he has an unpleasant experience in most restaurants because the noise levels make it impossible to hear what is being said at his own table (although this may be a device for keeping us out of those restaurants he doesn't particularly like).

As for the tingling sensation in his fingertips: this turned out to be immensely frustrating for me because David would drop things. He wanted to be helpful and put away dishes that had dried in the rack, but the tingling meant that he couldn't tell how well he was holding onto something, and that led to a lot of crashing and breaking. A Sleepytime tea mug that had been a Christmas present for my daughter. My favorite glass bowl. I pleaded with him to let me do that job, but I guess his pride was taking enough of a beating.

Did you know that many people don't finish their chemo

regimen? They become too sick or too fed up and they just don't show up anymore. I was surprised when the nurses told us this, but they were a little surprised themselves that David continued to show up even though his nausea was terrible. How scary.

AT THE GYM

While David was in chemo I worked out at the gym at the same time as a very nice woman did. She was in great shape and we often spoke to each other but she had one—to me—completely irritating flaw: she chewed gum as she exercised. One day I held my temper for about ten minutes and then I practically screamed at her, "Will you please stop cracking your gum!" I apologized immediately, explained that my husband was in chemo, and my penance was to finish working out in the presence of someone in front of whom I'd made an ass of myself.

Jeez, a little strung out?

IN THE MOST UNEXPECTED PLACES

Here's what helped me: when friends or just acquaintances would say they were praying for David. The praying itself was important, because I believe in its power, but I was also very touched by the concern people had for us. They thought about David and me and our daughter and they acted upon it. Sometimes the most unlikely person would say he was remembering us in his prayers, and I would be stunned that that person prayed.

I think this was important to me in another way, too. It let me know that, no matter how alone I felt as the wife of a sick man on chemo, I wasn't totally isolated.

WAITING TO GET A LIFE

Alice Kitselman

I've always had this hole deep inside, the question of what did I want to be when I grew up. What was my life going to look like, what was I going to be able to answer when that dreaded question came: "And what do you do?" I'd been waiting for inspiration; I'd been waiting for that moment of knowing. At the end of 2000 I was diagnosed with breast cancer and then after a battery of testing that hole inside showed up for real as a hole in my arm that was eaten away by a rare form of bone cancer. I thought I was going to die and I was never going to know what my life was all about.

This began the journey called cancer, and along with it a lot of waiting. Waiting for the results of tests, waiting for the end of grueling tests to be over, waiting for my blood pressure to come down enough to operate, waiting to heal and then to know what to do next. I didn't know which path to take; I didn't really know what to do or where to turn. I felt as if I just was making it all up, putting one foot in front of the other, moving toward healing, waiting to know when I was going to be pronounced "cured," finished, OK, here are your walking papers, you are now a graduate of cancer.

Today I sit with a group of other people who have all been touched by cancer in some manner, either directly as a survivor or as a mother, brother, wife of someone whom they cherished. We are sharing our stories through writing. On the wall in front of me is a painting of a bird that stirs up many emotions. This painting was formerly in the treatment room and now it is here haunting me. This painting was with me for my last four chemotherapy treatments. Somehow I just didn't like this painting. It reminded me of what I didn't have: freedom and hope. The painting is a burst of energy, a wild bird flying free, wings spread, exploding off the canvas. I am reminded of being nine or ten years old, my best friend Ginger and I in our underpants and plastic top hats. I would don a special Peter Max scarf and launch myself off the counter flying, flying free and wild for just one moment before I landed on the bed. My mother always wondered why she had to replace the mattresses so often.

Back in the hospital, I was chained, waiting for yet another cancer treatment to begin, this one being the drug called Taxol. I sat waiting for the nurse to be ready to inject me and all I could do was dwell on my fears. Why was it taking so long, shouldn't we have started by now, was something wrong with my last blood tests, what would this new drug do to me, what were the side effects going to be this time, will I make it through all this and come out OK at the other end? Here is this bird flying out of what looks like chaos to me. Wild slashing lines, explosions of eerie white and blues. While my life was full of chaos and fear, this bird was bursting through. This bird was going somewhere and I wasn't. I was trapped within a battle for my life. I was in limbo, I didn't feel safe, I was really damaged, I had cancer. I was about to be tethered to a slow, slow drip of a cocktail of drugs, a cocktail made of Taxol and steroids, antihistamine, anti-nausea medication, and who knows what else. My best hope for a cure, toxic medicine to ward off the cancer cells.

Now nine months since my last chemotherapy injection, here is this darn painting again! I'd wished I'd never have to see it again but here it is. This time I am inspired by it as it reminds me that from fear comes hope. While I was bald from chemotherapy I took a photograph of my bald head and sent it off to people all over the world with the instructions to decorate my bald head and send it back. Each week I would receive all kinds of versions that would delight me. I would receive wonderful collages of new and different versions of hair. Fanciful hats and new clothes. One even had a key stuck into my bald head. It definitely kept my mind off the cancer. I began to see a vision for the future; I want to make these post-cards into a book along with my cancer journey. Instead of feeling desolate, I now had a goal.

From a wounded life came direction and hope. Somewhere along the way I found myself and was able to say that cancer brought me a gift. I was no longer waiting to know what I was going to do in this life—I was doing it. I was being fully myself and full of dreams and desires that would no longer be put on hold. I was going to live and live fully. I know that sounds pretty corny but when one has faced the unknowingness that cancer brings, one wants to enjoy each moment in the now.

During that winter of treatments I received a gift basket in the mail from someone I didn't even know. This lovely gift was carefully packed full of items from her home state of Maine. With this basket came a ray of hope, caring and comfort that I was not alone. I later found out that my gift giver had also been through breast cancer. So after many months of grueling chemotherapy, thirty-three radiation treatments and a trip to New York City for the operation to remove the bone cancer from my arm, something magical happened. I believe that I found my calling: I created Dragonfly's Delights, a gift basket business to bring a ray of hope and tenderness to women who are in the midst of the dizzying journey of breast cancer. The time between diagnosis and treatment is filled with confusion and fear. I hope that the baskets I now make and have delivered to women going through what I did make a difference and bring a smile. This horrible disease has brought me a real gift of knowing, a calmness, a better sense of myself as who I am, the real me, extra weight, scars, tattoos and all.

A friend said to me recently that I was becoming my art. I really wasn't too sure what this meant. After all, I made art, I didn't see myself as art. But the truth is my bald head project really was a transformation of myself. I could and can really be as free as some of the portraits revealed. I can fly if I want to; fly into all the parts of myself I feel were missing or buried. Remember that hole in my arm? Well, I feel now it's been filled in, filled in with the love I needed all these years. I feel that somehow my art is my ability to create and change and move forward. I was able to get past the waiting, the not knowing, and just move ahead, be here now and move one step at a time. I'd always wanted a safe space to be free to be me and now I am finally in touch with a me that had been waiting, waiting to be discovered. Shoot, don't artists always wait to be discovered? I think I discovered myself!

I Call it My Cancer

Eleanor Castro

I call it my cancer because it is my cancer. It is nobody else's cancer but mine. It is not my husband's, it's not my mother's, it's not my kids'. It is my very own cancer. All to myself. Eleanor's Stage 4 colon cancer. Eleanor's Stage 4 colon cancer throughout the whole lymph system heading its way to the lungs and/or liver, say the doctors. Eleanor's colon cancer that is eventually going to kill her in a year or so.

So here is how it started. I was in northern California at my dying mother-in-law's bedside. She was dying of liver cancer. I spent day and night with her the last two weeks of her life, as did the rest of her very dedicated and loving family. She was this beautiful Salvadoran lady, a santita. She was the perfect mother, which makes my husband almost perfect with a few drawbacks. Anyway, I was so sick myself when I was with her. I would throw up. I would sweat. I had a chronic fever.

After she passed on, my husband took me to the emergency room in a little redneck suburbia-type town just south of San Francisco in the valley. The doctor who assisted me I honestly thought was as dumb as a soup sandwich. He had no clue. He spent one minute with me and told me that I had the flu. I left knowing that he was an incompetent idiot.

My husband had to go back to Santa Fe. My daughter Maria and I spent a couple days in San Francisco in the Mission District with an old Peace Corps friend of mine. When I wasn't throwing up or pooping in my pants I could spend a little time with her. My daughter and I then flew to Missoula, Montana, to visit my twin brother. I made sure I always had my diaper bag with me with new changes of clothes all the time. It was becoming a way of life for me. Throwing up, pooping in the old pants, sweating and feeling faint all of the time. We flew back to Santa Fe and we made sure that I sat right next to the toilet on the plane. This was August of 1999.

I went to the doctor here. She stuck something up my butt and said, Well, you are OK. No blood. From then on it was downhill. She prescribed medications for me to take after I ate so I would not throw up and my stomach would not hurt. So I added those pills to the old diaper bag.

Things started getting worse and worse. I was put in the hospital and was treated for irritable bowel syndrome. I got out of the hospital with more prescriptions to keep my stomach in line and from hurting. Throw 'em in the old diaper bag. I had to get a larger diaper bag to hold all of my daily necessities. The following week I went to the emergency room and was diagnosed with diverticulitus. I was put back in the hospital so they could give me more drugs. These drug companies are making big bucks. I was sent home from the hospital and I felt like I was going to die.

I went to a surgeon and I told him how bad I felt. He said, Eleanor, you do not have cancer. But let's be on the safe side and do a colonoscopy. So we did. Before we could even get the old rod up two inches you could see the tumor. Wrapped around my colon and the whole bowel area. So the doc who initially said I had irritable bowel syndrome calls me at six at night and says, Eleanor, you need to come into my office right away. I went in. He says, Eleanor, you have very aggressive colon cancer. I went home and my husband and I cried and cried. I felt this was my death sentence. I took a leave of absence from teaching in the Santa Fe Public Schools.

I immediately had surgery here in Santa Fe and started chemotherapy treatments. As I continued to get the chemo, I was bleeding rectally but the blood tests showed no tumor. The doc said, Eleanor, it is just a hernia. I went for another colonoscopy and sure enough. Another tumor. So I said, I am out of here. I set up everything and was at M.D. Anderson Cancer Center in Houston within three weeks. This was now late November 1999. I had the cutest—I mean *hot*—doctor. He was a Nazi type and would not let me talk to him or he would not talk to me. He knew everything. I figured since he hangs out with a lot of colons every day I would trust him. He cut me open. Found me with cancer throughout my lymph system all the way up into my aorta. He could not touch the cancer that close to my aorta. He also said that sooner if not later it would travel into my lungs and/or liver, and within a year I would be history.

So I was recuperating in the hospital in Houston. Saying to myself, this cancer is not going to kill me. I am not ready to leave this planet and they are not ready for me up there yet. I have two young teenage daughters and a young husband. So I lived on the assumption that I was not going to die and here I am. I ain't dead yet.

The closest I came to death in Houston was when my twin brother was pushing me all around Holcombe Boulevard in the wheelchair. I fell out of the wheelchair into the main boulevard. Pajamas, gas mask. I wish I had a picture of that. My brother was laughing so hard he could not get it together to get me out of the street. It was really very funny.

So I am back from Houston and starting megadoses of chemotherapy. I was fat, bald and I felt like shit but I wasn't going to die. I finished my treatments. I picked up fibromyalgia, which is an autoimmune system disease which comes with my personality and my past health and emotional history. But I ain't dead and I can live with fibromyalgia. I have to pop a pain pill every so often but oh well.

In September of 2001 I was stricken with three strangulated hernias and ended up having eight hours of emergency surgery and a week and a half in intensive care. I was two months with a very large open wound which had to be taken care of by visiting nurses. I looked like a cut of beef just getting ready to be grilled. This last surgery was not related to the other surgery but it does make it surgery number eight.

I am now a happy and smiling retired public school teacher and have been hanging with my family and friends for the past two years. My hair is back, I lost some weight, I still hurt but I don't have cancer and I am still on this planet.

CAN A WOMAN WITH ONE BREAST AND NO HAIR BE SEXY?

Judi Jaquez

I don't recall exactly when I first noticed in the mirror that my right nipple pulled, turning outwards. I don't recall exactly when I first felt the hard little lump. Like in pregnancy something started growing in my body with a plan all its own. I would be the observer, the learner through the changes, treatments and the outcome to follow. The mammogram wasn't definitive, so ultrasound followed. The faces of the technician and radiologist held pity, their demeanor discomfort. But did they tell me? *No!* I had to wait a week for the surgeon to look at the same film and immediately say, "Why do they always leave the bad news for me? It's cancer." I couldn't hear anymore. Dazed. Robotic. Home. Tears. Wine. Phone calls.

Suddenly I was a patient. My life was taken over by doctors' appointments, tests, picking up prescriptions, registering for procedures, filling out their forms where I'd always marked "No." No high blood pressure, no diabetes, no, no, no. Now I mark "yes" to cancer! Can it be true?

I also became a student of cancer, its treatments and its terminology: invasive lobular carcinoma, sentinel node procedure, modified mastectomy, trans-flap reconstruction, breast prosthesis. Everything is a statistic: twenty percent chance of local recurrence, fifty percent risk of metastases, forty to sixty percent increased survival.

And then, so quickly, I was admitted, prepped, incised, sutured, bandaged, discharged and at home like a little girl, being cared for by my seventy-eight-year-old mother and eighty-four-year-old father. For the first time in over two years I felt no responsibility for my job—The Job from Hell. Just sleep, rest, eat and then repeat.

On the morning my parents were to leave, I finally allowed myself to look at my full front view in the mirror. It wasn't the same as looking down at the incision across my chest to check the healing. There I was with part of me gone, just lumpy ribs and a purple-red slash where my lovely breast had been. I heard screams of rage and anguished animal-like sobs, my chest heaved, my shoulders shook. Later I told the surgeon, "I've been hating you for taking my breast." She responded, "That's okay. Now give me a hug."

Losing the boob took me by surprise. I wasn't going to be caught unaware when the hair went too. My sister, Dotti, and I planned a grand shopping spree on the day of my first chemo to buy a replacement boob and wig. "Hey, Doc! Just write that prescription for the prosthesis. I may want a penis instead of a breast when I get to the parts store."

As for chemotherapy—therapy is surely a misnomer—potent poisons, so toxic they harden the veins as they touch their walls. The chemicals penetrate the tissue, leaking into your taste and smell— metallic, chemical. They say the chemicals can't cross the blood/ brain barrier. Then what takes over your brain, making familiar words disappear, eliminating decision-making powers, letting one observe things without recording a memory of it?

And the symptoms worsen with each round of chemo ("rounds" they call them, like in prizefights). Something affected my nervous system, making my skin crawl, my body agitated, unable to sit, to stand. I could only pace, thinking, "I can't take this!"

But that's over! Now I'm left with radiation fatigue. Tireder than tired, bone-tired! Isn't it a pity that just when my brain returned to duty, filled with pent-up plans, creativity and enthusiasm, my body is on strike?

Cancer has made me fearless. What are other fears compared to the fear of dying, the fear of being really sick? I've overcome the fear of exposing my needy and vulnerable side. I've learned to ask for help. I surrendered the fear of really letting love in. I rejoice in letting people love me in whatever form it's offered. Mom loves me by cooking and cleaning. Numerous cafeteria ladies I supervised in El Paso send me cards, say they pray for me, thank me for something they perceive I've given them. Audrey, my neighbor, whose name I didn't even know, came over with a home-cooked meal after every chemo. One employee (who was rude and threatening when we met) now gave me hugs and an Avon cancer bear. I just soak in all the love and caring.

Cancer has also shut up my inner critic. I finally have the courage and words to talk back to it as fiercely as it talks to me. "Shut up! So I'm not doing it your way—perfectly—I'm doin' it! If it's not perfect I'll try again. Fuck you!"

Cancer has revealed to me my own preciousness. I've often abandoned myself in the past. But this time I've cared for myself gently, patiently and lovingly. I've gifted myself in small ways from lavender baths to comfy clothes, to weekends of videos and naps and wrenching tears. I've admired myself for my courage and honesty and strength. I've accepted that my life has meant something to others even if I never really knew it before.

I no longer accept perpetual worry, irrational fears. If they show up I can say, "But I want to buy a convertible, and live in the house of my dreams, and learn to fly-fish!" (Where did that come from?) And why not? I've got cancer!

And it's given me such a good excuse to not do what I don't want. "I'm just not up to it—you know, the cancer."

I don't know exactly when I started to accept that woman in the mirror with the shadow of eyebrows returning, sleek charcoal and silver hair covering the shapely crown, and an out-of-balance chest as *me*. But I like me much better this way! So much more open to possibilities. I visualize creating my unique home and know I'll make it happen. The Job from Hell now lets me feel and express caring for women and children and see them all being more than they think they can be.

I made the cabinet in my room that had become my "sick kit" into my art cabinet. And I'm starting to think, maybe I'll have a lover someday. Do you just say as you're getting undressed, "By the way, I seem to have lost my right breast somewhere"? Or do you just strap on a sensual, exotic silken concoction—stuffed, beaded, sequined, maybe tasseled—and not say a word? Can a woman with no hair and one breast be sexy?

MaryAna Eames

Today I realize why I have been asked to be part of this book. I need to learn how to ask and remember how to cry. I realize that although my victory over two bouts of cancer has provided me with a deep insight into my being and my needs, the tribulations of four years of cancer have taken their toll. I have learned to be a better person and help others with cancer, but I have not learned how to be a better friend to myself.

My emotional and spiritual healing is essential. I know it requires a lot of time and silence, but countless hours of silent reflection have taught me that the first step in healing is asking. I must learn how to ask. If I do not ask soon, I will fade away—and not from cancer.

Asking would enable me to better communicate with my family and help them understand me better. I love them so much—my husband, Peter, and our two sons, Evan, age eighteen, and Laine, age twelve. They were so brave and so scared when I had cancer. They all took care of me when I was sick and helped my physical resurgence. But now, my trials with cancer are demanding that my family must also understand me better and see the "real me," and the support I need. They must understand how I feel under my shell. But I have not learned how to ask for support—not even from them.

I worry about not being around to raise my children into adulthood. I want so much to be there for them—to help them in their developmental, psychological and spiritual paths. I especially worry about Evan. Like me, Evan is a fragile but loving individual. He really needs the warmth of a mother's touch. He needs guidance, especially now as he moves into adulthood. Cancer interrupted our warm embraces and had us both running scared. Cancer produced anger and frustration in Evan and a guilt that maybe the cancer was there because of something he had done. It is taking time for both of us to learn how to reconnect and dispel the fears, which still linger—fears that the cancer will come back and destroy the last vestiges of everything we are trying to rebuild. I also hope that I will be around to see Laine grow into a secure adulthood. Laine is a special, compassionate person—and we need more time to spend quality time together doing fun things that will nurture his soul and maximize his potential. Finally, I worry about leaving my wonderful husband alone. I dream so much of growing old with him, toothless, silly and forgetful, surfing at Carpenteria Beach in our seventies.

Now, two years into a second remission from my cancer, I am striving to cleanse my soul and freshen my spirit. I wish I could have a good cry. Cancer has forced me to be so strong over the last four years. Strong for myself, strong for my family and friends, and strong for other cancer patients I have helped. I have been so strong that I have forgotten how to cry. If I ask for help when I descend to my darkest hour and grapple for a comforting hand, I am afraid that no one will be there for me. If I asked for help, I wonder if my friends, family, and others would understand that I need help and that I want help. They have always viewed me as independent, a solid pillar of strength and accomplishment, the self-starter who requires no assistance or support from others. I wonder if they are able to see the *new me*—the one that really needs their support—the one that must have their support.

My family and friends just don't understand when I am trying to help myself. They understand perfectly when I help others. At these times, when I am giving, there are many receivers. However, when I am in need, the room becomes very empty, and I am left alone again with no one to comfort me or understand what I am going through. Cancer challenged me on every level. I had to become a warrior overnight just to survive. Now I have forgotten how to show my needs to others. I have forgotten how to ask.

I remember when I was first diagnosed with cancer; the four *Spirits of the Medicine* appeared to me during a visualization session conducted by my therapist to help me stick to a difficult chemotherapy regimen. These spirits turned out to be my internal guides—they encompass everything I am and everything I must do to heal myself. I remember when they first appeared in a magnificent parade of light—each the color of the chemotherapy medicine they represented. Adriamycin—the brave red warrior with flashing eyes, Bleomycin—a steel blue superhero with bulging muscles and a powerful, piercing stare. And then there is the beautiful fairy, Vincristine—with her gentle visage, adorned in a glimmering satin gown trimmed with gold. She looks a lot like Glenda, the good witch from *The Wizard of Oz*. Every time I see her she is smiling back at me, reassuring me that the cancer will not come back. And finally, there is Dacarbazine—the most powerful spirit of the medicines—a handsome, mysterious character with his black leather jacket and black silk shirt and trousers, he moves cursively through my psyche like a benevolent Johnny Depp. These spirits are always with me. They assured me that I would not die and that I would emerge from my cancer. They told me that they would be with me forever to guide and protect me. They are with me every day and every moment, guiding me to reach inside and feel—just learn how to feel again.

Cancer has forced me to be so strong over the last four years. Strong for myself, strong for my family and friends and strong for other cancer patients I have helped. If I ask for help when I descend to my darkest hour and grapple for a comforting hand, I am afraid that no one will be there for me. Now, two years into a second remission from my cancer, I wish I could have a good cry.

I used to be able to cry when things built up inside me. Crying was a wonderful relief that renewed my spirit and calmed my emotions. Today, my armor is too heavy and I have forgotten how to cry. Instead, I don my hard and glistening intellectual armor and march into some external activity such as charity fundraisers for children with cancer, or some other cause where I can forget about my own problems. To others, my protective armor is convincing, dashing and attractive. It assures others how strong and accomplished I am. It validates the perpetual visage that I need no support. I am invincible, a staunch pillar of helping others, the "model cancer survivor."

Moving On

Barbara Ness

I'm breathless…feel like I'm running a race. I've been moving…I mean literally, actually, right in the midst of this writing workshop! My nails are broken, I have bruises all over my body, my back is out…I'm exhausted. I wonder…could all this be a metaphor? For moving on in my life? Especially over the last six months, since my fourth diagnosis of retroperitoneal liposarcoma? (That's a cancer in the abdominal/pelvic area—relatively rare.)

Racing…to set up surgery while checking on clinical trials, because the surgeries, the only treatment known for this cancer, are taking their toll on my body and energy.

Racing to California to finish my Imagery Therapy Certification Training (that's something like hypnotherapy).

Racing to Florida with my son, at his request, to reintroduce him to his roots and relatives. I wonder if he thought I might die before we could do that? I'll admit that when friends tried to convince me to postpone that trip, I cried, realizing that if we didn't go then I might never have the chance to give my son that legacy.

Then racing back to Santa Fe for November surgery and recuperation. Now the moving on really begins.

I finally made the heart-wrenching decision to leave my marriage, the husband of my mature choice, the man I thought was the love of my life and my partner forever; to leave my spacious El Dorado home with the stunning sunsets.

What a scary decision, to choose to live only with myself in a rental house, parting with many of my beloved possessions...all because I believe it is so critical for my ultimate healing.

I've known others who have left relationships or been abandoned by loved ones because of cancer, but I never thought I'd be one to leave. I wasn't abandoned by anyone, at least physically. Those who "went away" when they were faced with my recurrences left emotionally.

My husband was one of these—at least it seemed like it to me. He detached, pulled into himself, wasn't "there for me" in the ways I needed him to be, even though he said and thought he was. He didn't seem to want to know what I was feeling, about my fears and doubts, what was going on in my mind. We didn't even touch anymore.

I remember when I met him ten years ago. He was the answer to my dreams and prayers. He was loving, funny, intelligent, Jewish. (I was leaning toward the Jewish faith, and besides, Jewish men are supposed to make good husbands, they say.) He liked to be with me. We shared lots of interests, talked about everything, and had great sex.

But gradually, that all drifted away. The first cancer in 1995 wasn't so bad. We stuck together, faced our mortality together, and realizing we would both die someday, we chose to grasp life with both hands and made the joint decision to move to Santa Fe.

Then things really began to fall apart. What went first? I don't even remember anymore.

He became more and more angry. Even his humor became dark and angry. He became obsessed with business and money. Maybe these were things he could handle emotionally, while he watched me undergoing a second and then a third surgery. After all, he had already lost one wife to cancer. Our marriage became an empty shell, with none of the benefits that marriage offers...only the responsibilities remained.

I tried...God, did I try...but I just couldn't fix it. And now, I'm the one who is going away...away from the loneliness of that marriage...away from the man who used to love me...perhaps still does...but who can't share life with me as I need to share it.

It's the death of a dream for me. Going away...sadly...but with a new sense of adventure. Perhaps I've been moving toward this point all my life. Perhaps it's a new launching point for me. Perhaps now is the time to love myself.

CROSSROADS

Argos MacCallum

While cancer has never threatened my life beyond the inconvenience of having spots on my face frozen off every eight months and once a small piece cut out of my right temple, it is certainly on a first-name basis with my family. My younger brother and father are under the same sort of surveillance. My twenty-six-year-old niece had a lump removed from her breast, which was mercifully nonmalignant. But my mother and youngest brother, Reid, fought losing battles with cancer at the ages of fifty-three and forty-three.

Reid and I were living at the old ranch, which had become a small, dusty community in the shadow of the Cerrillos Hills. My wife, Corinna, lived there too. It was a late summer afternoon with a whiff of fall, of freedom from the searing heat, that extra smell of color in the air. I was watering the Russian olive trees by the flagstone path. Reid was sitting outside on the ground at some distance in front of the old stables he and I had converted into living quarters. Sitting with him was K, whose life was entwined with his in some fashion I had never understood and whose presence always put me on edge. K had been my other brother Bruce's wife and had helped raise his daughter from a previous relationship. Bruce's daughter could not abide K at all. Nor could Bruce's new wife, Joanie, who lived with Bruce and their two very young daughters in town in a state of incredible happiness.

Reid and K sat there on the ground in this fabulous afternoon and looked from a distance like they were part of an eighteenth-century Dutch pastoral painting juxtaposed in a strange desert setting. But there was a bitter acid frisson, a strange whiff that entered my nostrils and set off a reluctant alarm.

Suddenly a sharp twang, a strident warning. Some sort of threat in K's voice that reached my ears although the words were unintelligible. My head snapped in their direction. My heart sank as I realized that this was one of those moments where the great wing of the future brushed against the cheek of the present moment and all was altered in a second. And I was cowed, frozen, unable to move. I reached down to move the hose as anger planted a seed in me. I knew somehow that K had thrown a shovel of dirt on the embers of Reid's heart, had tightened the noose on his hopes of beginning a relationship with a woman who really wanted to be part of his life.

Reid had gone to his twentieth high school reunion and met L, who was now a successful advertising executive in New York. She was part of a prominent family in Tesuque. L and Reid connected and laughed over anecdotes from school days. They arranged a date and quickly found a common ground and a mutual respect and love Reid had probably never known. Within a week she had invited him to join her in New York and find a new sort of life.

All this I found out from Joanie later. She had had some beers with Reid when he came to the house to take a shower after a day of plastering before his date with L and said his eyes were suffused with a light she had never seen before.

And in this moment on the ground in front of the converted stables, that light evaporated, shooting through his fingers into the air like frightened hummingbirds.

Reid and K were now inextricably linked for the rest of his life.

Not long after the three of us began to build our own houses on a piece of land we had been able to buy because most of my mother's side of the family had passed away in a very short time. The sale of the two-story white clapboard family house that Uncle Charlie had built in Winchester, Virginia, right after the Civil War brought in just enough money for the land and some building materials.

After such a rootless childhood, my brothers and I wanted a solid family base that Bruce's daughters would inherit. After doing construction jobs all our lives we could now build for ourselves, and we jumped in feet first. Reid grumbled that Bruce and I had nabbed the best building sites, but he finally chose a site for his straw bale house on the other side of the grassy draw that ran through the property, at a fair distance from our houses. A site that had fabulous views.

He grudgingly let us help him with the foundations, which were carved out of seemingly endless rock and then the post-and-beam structure required by the New Mexico state building code for straw bale houses. The posts were from an old telephone line that crossed the Cerrillos Hills and hadn't been used for twenty years or so. We went out on Easter Sunday with an old Dodge pickup truck and a two-man saw and lineman's pliers—we could have used a chain saw but that would have made too much noise—and we cut down a mile and a half of telephone poles. Just enough for the post-and-beam structure.

Bruce and I worked hard on our places—a house for Bruce's family (that was the priority, obviously) and a tiny studio for me. They were unfinished but livable. Corinna had a small studio we had built on her property next door. I wore down a path in the scanty grass that I could practically run from one end to the other with my eyes closed.

But Reid stayed in his quarters on the ranch for much of that time, reading books and fighting depression. Only as winter approached did he start on finishing his house, and when his money ran out he borrowed a dilapidated trailer from a friend and put it on the land to live in and damn near froze to death with his cat.

When it warmed up we put a tin roof on the post-and-beam structure. Then Reid installed the door and window frames and began stacking the straw bales himself. He didn't want any help with that part. The progress was painstakingly slow. He secured each bale with lengths of the steel tension wire from the old telephone line. When the course of bales rose over his head he would climb day after day up rickety old ladders he had scrounged from somewhere with the bales balanced on his shoulders.

K decided then that she and Reid were no longer soulmates. She made plans to move to Hawaii. But she figured she couldn't go until Reid got some medical advice for the black oozing hole that had been on his chest for a few months. Only after the straw bales were in place did he make an appointment.

A calm, cool November day, a pale blue sky leaning toward noon. Pink Floyd suddenly blasted at top volume out of Reid's trailer. I went outside and stared across the draw.

"What the hell is that all about?" I asked Joanie, who was walking my way.

"You know about the black hole in his chest?"

I knew he had said his chest itched a lot, but I attributed that to the straw getting inside the muscle shirt he always wore and sticking to the sunscreen he used all the time. I didn't know about the black hole.

"Well, it's cancer," she said, and disappeared.

Reid was dancing madly around his tiny trailer, which hadn't been cleaned in weeks. I think he justified all the newspapers on the floor as extra insulation. The door was open. I called his name. He slowly, reluctantly came to a standstill.

"Stage 3 melanoma. My chances aren't good."

We stared at each other in silence. I knew we were both thinking about our mother's rapid decline and death. Her surgery had been quick. The doctors opened up her abdomen, poked around and wrote her off.

"Look, you can't stay in this damn trailer again this winter. Take my studio. I could move in with Corinna. Her studio is tight, but we'll cozy up. Bruce and I can help you with your house. And we'll help you fight the cancer." I clasped his hand and then walked away with a huge sinking feeling.

The three of us hung doors and windows and built some interior walls. The last thing Reid did before he got too weak to work was lay the brick floor of his bedroom. Bruce and I put up the ceiling, plastered the walls and set up one of the antique beds from the family house back east. It was the one in which our mother as a small child had nearly died of diphtheria one night during the Depression.

Reid and K took a two-week vacation to Hawaii and then came back to fight the disease. There was no insurance, of course. K quietly appointed herself primary caregiver and took control of his finance and appointment book. She made strategic decisions concerning treatment, with some input from our father but none from the rest of us. We were more than happy to run errands, but felt increasingly marginalized. Reid and K made trips to Houston and Phoenix for consultations, but the information was contradictory and bewildering, especially from the sidelines. Hospice became part of the equation. A Tibetan lama and doctor came to the straw bale house one day. Groups of people prayed in the house.

The radiation treatment had run its course. Reid and K arrived early for the appointment to consult on the prognosis. The doctor had not yet had time to study the report. Scanning it, the doctor said that the treatment had been effective. Only a few tumors remained that, although temporarily enlarged, would most likely disappear quickly with further treatment. The doctor went on vacation the next day. K, who had been trained as a nurse, felt she ought to take a closer look at the report. She got a copy from the hospital. It said Reid was riddled with tumors. What had been said and what had been heard didn't jibe.

The fight went out of Reid. He became bedridden. There was still vague talk of an alternative cure in Mexico, but we all knew he couldn't even get on a plane. Now was the time for the hushed tones around the straw bale house. Certainly his music—Pink Floyd, Little Feat, Cream, Bonnie Raitt, the Pretenders—which had been sporadic up to that point, ceased to play. K insisted on peace and quiet.

Reid became paranoid that Bruce and I would refuse to bury him on the land. I knew it was that odd-brother-out situation again. Three always breaks down into two against one. And most often as kids Reid was the one.

I took a video of a spot on the edge of the grassy draw nestled between a small rock outcrop and a stand of piñon. I panned up to the straw bale house on the opposite side glowing in the late afternoon sun like a golden temple. A fine resting place. But Reid was gone on morphine and couldn't focus on the television screen.

The next day the play I was in closed. And the next day was summer solstice and Bruce's birthday. We didn't celebrate.

Around five in the afternoon an exhausted K asked if one of us would sit in the chair by the bed. I said yes. Reid was awake. His mouth was so dry he couldn't talk. Any talk would have seemed ludicrous anyway. After a few minutes I asked if he would like a little music. He looked at me with a conspiratorial gleam in his eye. I'm sure that's what it was. I stood up and put on Pink Floyd's *Piper at the Gates of Dawn*. After a few minutes he indicated that he wanted to stand up. I helped him out of bed.

There, in my arms, in the first embrace we shared in God knows how long, he said, "I'm very, very sorry, folks," and died.

We lowered him into the grave the next day just before sunset—in his boots, blue jeans, and Pink Floyd T-shirt. He had also requested his glasses, just in case he needed them. No satin, no coffin. Just a few mementos in his pockets and some flowers in his hands. He was traveling light.

2 A.M.

Judy Kiphart

2 a.m. Anxiety…worry…panic. There is nothing I can do about anything, no control. Is that what's so terrifying? No control? I can't do or fix anything at two a.m. It just has to *be*. Thoughts creep in and there is nothing to distract me. Worries over little things become so big, so overwhelming. During my cancer treatments the panic was so intense—there's no way to know how things will work out. My God, I have cancer. How can that be? What does it mean? What will happen? My prognosis is good, but I still wish that all the cancer markers they tested for were not positive. It lurks in the back of my mind. Do I only have five years left? How could that be? I'm supposed to live until my eighties or nineties like my grandparents. What if I don't? What will happen? What would it be like without me? Would I be missed? Have I made a difference being here? What should I be doing? All these questions. Panic over daily things—our pets, work and bills, panic over my husband, Don, and our son, Daniel.

I loved being pregnant with Daniel. I wasn't sure about the delivery part—some people tell such horror stories. But I did it and what a high. Everything appeared fine even though he was five weeks early. The joy and excitement of having this baby! Then the doctor wakes me in the middle of the night. Daniel's having trouble breathing and the doctor wants to do a spinal tap. I had to sign the form for the procedure. In such a short time I had such extreme emotions, from such incredible elation after his birth to the terror of losing him that night. The test results came back OK and after ten days in the hospital he was able to come home.

Daniel is seventeen now and will be a senior in high school. Almost ready to leave the nest. Where has the time gone? As irritating as it can be, I'll miss the way he jumps out from behind a door and scares me. Or the way he does that head-butting thing, just inches from my face. But we always laugh and I get a hug.

When he was little, we'd bake together. He loved cracking the eggs. Then we'd spend several minutes laughing and pulling egg shells out of the batter. He went through the *Ghostbusters* phase. He gave all three of us *Ghostbusters* names. He was Ray, Don was Egan and I was Dr. Venkman. This was funny at home, but I'll never forget the look one woman gave me when he called me Dr. Venkman at the store.

I remember one of our long car trips to Indiana. After reading a book about space aliens, he made paper antennae and stuck them in my hair. Then we forgot about them and stopped for lunch. I wondered why people at the restaurant were giving me such strange looks. As soon as we got in the car, I saw those antennae sticking up out of my hair in the mirror.

I love our family time together. Daniel and I like to garden. When we lived in Denver, we would go to the Botanic Garden's plant and book sale every Mother's Day. Don never minded all the plants we brought home, as long as it didn't mean yet another digging and rototilling project for him. We've always had cats and a dog. We also went through the shorter-lifespan pets—the turtle, the toad, the lizards. Every week we'd make the trip to the pet store to buy crickets for them to eat.

After my diagnosis, I told my friend in Denver how Daniel joked about getting me a rainbow-colored clown wig when I lost my hair from the chemo. And how he would rub my bald head for good luck before exams. I still remember the relief in her voice when she said how glad she was to hear that the Kipharts were still laughing, she knew we'd get through this.

Daniel is an individual. If he's interested in something, he does it. He doesn't worry about what other people think. I'm relieved that I didn't pass that Midwest trait on to him—worrying about what other people think.

I grew up in a small Midwest town. I remember the weekly piano lessons with Bessie, the formal piano recitals, picnics at the park, catching lightning bugs, Sunday-afternoon drives and stopping to get ice cream on the way home. This is also where I learned to worry about what other people think. We were taught to be nice, to do the "right" thing, to follow the "rules."

What a crock! I followed the rules and still got breast cancer. I didn't smoke or use birth control pills, I breast-fed Daniel, did yoga, and had a healthy diet. All the things that are supposed to help prevent you from getting breast cancer.

Cancer has shaken my faith. What is faith and what does it mean to me? I first really questioned my faith after the miscarriage. When Daniel was in fourth grade we found out I was pregnant. After all the years of trying to get pregnant again, this was a shock. As the shock wore off, we all got excited about this new baby. At ten weeks, I miscarried. During those days of bleeding and not knowing if this pregnancy would continue, my family prayed for us. My niece's Sunday school class prayed for the baby. Have faith that everything will be okay. I lost the baby and wondered what I did wrong—was my faith not strong enough?

I no longer believe that if I follow the rules and have faith nothing bad will happen to me or my family. For me, these days, faith means that as things happen in my life, whatever I need to get through it will be provided for me. When I can't express all my fears to my family, a friend has always been there to listen. When I've worried about money, another work project has always turned up.

When I worry about all the future "what ifs," I remember how past "what ifs" have always been worked out during the day. I want to remember these things when the panic starts in at two a.m.

I'm not up as often now as I was during treatment. Sometimes the memories and fears wake me up and overwhelm me. I don't know what to do. I don't know how much time I have. No one knows how long we'll be here. Cancer pulled me out of the false sense of security that I'm guaranteed to grow old. I don't know what this next phase of my life will be. I want to grow old with Don, to see what Daniel does with his life and be there when he needs us. I want to be a grandma and share fun times with my grandchildren. I want all this, but know there are no guarantees for any of it.

So, sometimes, I write in my journal and pray. Sometimes I'll turn the TV on quietly for background distraction. Sometimes I just sit it out and wait for the light of day. I have an advertisement for local artist Phyllis Kapp's annual show at her gallery. Don cut it out for me because he knows how much I like her work. I love the picture of her watercolor in this ad, especially the title—*All My Memories Are Happy Tonight*. This reminds me of all the times my faith has been there. And I wait for the sun to come up.

THE TIME OF MY LIFE

Nancy Henry

The summer before my sixteenth birthday my mother was diagnosed with breast cancer. That is the first memory I have of time consciously seeming important to me. I had never thought about it much before then. The years of my childhood had just gone by. I remember things happening, and mostly I remember the things that happened which seemed to underscore the endless unhappiness that defined my life. I remember when I was three and four I got to spend every day with Roger Lowman. He lived three houses down and he was my soul mate and I loved him so, and then just before I was five my family moved away—across town— and I never saw Roger again. And I remember my loneliness then that had no end in time. I remember when I was six and I told my sister I hated her and my mother told me that telling someone you hate them means you wish they would die and I remember the guilt that took root in my heart then and it, also, had no end in time. And I remember Charlie Frost, who made me sit on his lap sometimes when I was eight and made me rub his penis while he rubbed my labia and stuck his fingers in my vagina. I couldn't tell my mother and father about what he was doing to me because he was their best friend, so my disgust and fear and shame just got put into the big pot of feelings that got lost in time.

I remember Wanda Hardister in the sixth grade who had the cutest body and the tightest jeans—and they were real Levi's—but I was fat and wore regular ugly jeans, not Levi's, and I watched her from inside myself and the years went by and I just watched life from an endlessly isolated and lonely spot.

I guess that time just actually seemed like something to get through, not something that had any substance or any worth of its own. And then my mom got cancer. I don't know what all it meant to her, she never talked about it, none of us ever talked about it. But I heard somebody say clearly right at first that if the cancer wouldn't come back for five years then she would be okay. I don't know who said that. I don't know if it was really said. But I believed it. And suddenly time had great meaning. My life wasn't meaningless drifting anymore. We just had to get through five years. I had started smoking six months before that and I made a deal with God that I would stop if He'd be sure and let my mom make it through those five years and be okay. I thought that might be one way I could help. And I remember for a long time ticking off the months on a little calendar I kept on a nail in my closet. And I remember that this five-year period almost seemed like a tangible block of something I chipped away at—with the treasure at the center waiting for me. And the five years did go by and my mother was okay and that five-year anniversary was a big day for me. I smiled the whole day and took such deep breaths and felt so relieved. And I quit counting the days on the calendar. Then six months later I went home to visit her from college and I was lying with my head in her lap—that was something we did, I would lay my head in her lap and she would stroke my hair and that was always such a comforting and nurturing experience for me. And she was telling me that she thought she might have a touch of the flu, that she wasn't feeling quite right. And then she belched—twice—and her breath smelled like death—and I knew that the cancer had come back and that she would die. And again the concept of time became a focal point for me—this time as some progressive entity which would end with the death of my mother—and I did believe that my life would be over when my mother died.

My mother did die, but of course my life did continue, and the years have gone by and I have had my ups and downs and my ins and outs and, again, I quit thinking about the concept of time. Then six months ago I was diagnosed with breast cancer and I'm thinking a lot again about time. The facts about this cancer of mine are that it seems to be a pretty good cancer and the probability that it will recur is relatively low. But it is cancer, and that puts me into a whole new category than I've ever been in before. And I think I will never be quite the same again. I think that I have been given a gift here— the gift of time. I don't know why I have been given this gift, and I feel confused about what it means. I find that most people I know think of me as "over it," as having the cancer behind me now, and they want me to be ready and able to get on with my life, to "resume" my life.

But it isn't quite that easy. I just keep thinking about what does it mean, what does the amazing gift of time mean, how can I utilize it most fully? I try to keep my eyes and ears and heart open so I can understand more. I try to meditate about it. I take a walk every morning and while I'm walking I meditate and pray about my experience of this gift. And I feel I ought to be getting closer to some clarity for myself. I feel I ought to be getting more to where my gratitude for this gift defines my experience, where my thankfulness leaves me calm in a centered and ongoing way. Instead, the same old things happen. Like the other day, I was walking on the dirt roads by my house, feeling in tune with the beauty around me and grateful for my life and just about as centered as I could possibly imagine myself being. And a guy comes zooming by me in his car going about 45 and his car kicks up clouds of dust which immediately envelope me and I swing around and start jumping up and down, giving him the finger and yelling, "Fuck you, asshole!!!" From centered peacefulness to fury in two seconds. I guess I haven't quite figured out what this all means yet. And maybe some things will never change. I feel anxiety, and I feel confusion, but I also find I am asking myself a lot of questions and the questions feel important to me as I head out on this path. Will there be enough time for me, for all of us, to be who we want to be? Will we be caught short? Will we kid ourselves about what time is left to us and then be disappointed? Is there time enough for me to forgive those I want to forgive? Is there time enough for me to let go of my guilt about the ways I've sometimes lived, about the people I've deeply and knowingly hurt?

Will there be time to see enough sunsets and sunrises? Will I reach the day when I believe my images of those colors fill my whole heart and I don't have room to see any more? Will I reach the day when I no longer believe I need to hear Patti La Belle slide into her highest note again? Will there be time to see all the dances my David has in his heart? Will I have time to let the people I love know—as much as they need to know and as much as I need to tell them—how much I do love them, how much they mean to me, how important their being in my life has been. Will there be enough time to tell others how I feel—about everything—and not be afraid to look weak or foolish or dependent or odd? Will there be enough time to kiss my dogs Annie and Lem Dean as much as they need to be kissed? Will there be time to clearly and thoroughly tell my god how thankful I am for the love I have felt and do feel, for the life I have had and do have, for the people who have participated in my life with me? Will there be time to let go of the jealousy I feel for others who seem to have that "easier go of it"? That jealousy leaves me feeling so ugly and so small. I seem to believe that maybe some-day I can let it go—but will there be time to do it—especially if I keep seeing it as something for the future? Can I care about those who trespass against me? Can I see that others are human and falli-ble and frail just like I am? Will there be time to just let myself feel others' humanity and love them for being in this life just like I am—all of us creatures who need compassion and love and each other? I don't know if there will be time. I hope so.

Dedicated to Bill Abdallah, Barry Saltzman, and Mike Robbins—three of the good guys who fell too early.

I Wish I'd Noticed That My Body Was a Temple

Blythe Jane Richfield

I had cancer of the sphincter muscle. Sphincter…it really rolls off the tongue so delicately, doesn't it? Sometimes I wonder what it would have been like to have a cancer that affected a part of the body that we're more used to talking about. Not that the cancer would have been any easier to deal with. But let's face it, we get nervous when we have to pronounce the planet Uranus. Or, is it *yer anus…?* But no, we don't talk about our shit. And we certainly don't have a natural inclination to use the word *sphincter* in any of our day-to-day conversations. The always-descriptive word *asshole* is pretty acceptable. But then, since mine's been removed, I no longer qualify.

Still, the sphincter muscle was the target of my cancer. So the surgeons went to work to save my body by extracting my colon piece by piece and replacing it with a colostomy and finally an ileostomy. Three months later, they removed my rectum and began the administration of chemotherapy and radiation. Radiation. That invisible ray of destructive fire was focused directly into my pelvis one day, and shot straight up between my legs, into my vagina the next, every day for thirty-five days. After that particular assault, I was left with saving my soul. And that one endeavor became the most challenging and most important aspiration of my life—for it was the catalyst that began to teach me what it meant to savor this one life.

After eleven surgeries, chemotherapy and radiation, I was left with so much vaginal scar tissue that the act of intercourse become one of my life's impossibilities. Now, I'm not embarrassed to admit that I like intercourse! After all of the loss…no colon, no rectum, no babies, and now, no intercourse? It was simply unacceptable. And so I prayed. Of course, I also cried and denied and felt like I might go insane. But dammit, I prayed. For eleven celibate years I prayed, "Dear God, this body that I have been given: a plastic bag in which to face my shit, and a beautiful Yoni with no room left for entry, please God, *please* help me to understand the nature and expression of true love. Not sex, God. I know sex. You went through the sixties with me, after all. I need your help so that I might experience the true essential nature of love." And that was the most difficult question— for how would I find the wisdom and courage to accept the limitations of this war-torn body, let alone find another to dare to make that journey and meet my body and life as a true expression of the love of God?

And then, as prayers are sometimes wont to do, my petition was answered. Michael. My beautiful, brilliant, romantic Michael. We met at midnight one autumn in Vermont. We talked for hours. Beckett's *Waiting for Godot*, and Michael's smile were the only things I remembered about that evening. He left for his home in New York the next morning, while I boarded a plane back to Santa Fe. Three months followed with letters and phone calls. He wanted to come and visit. How was I to shed my skin and prepare him for that which he could not have been expecting?

I wrote him a story about a girl who had lived my life. It was my own grim fairy tale. I was the rejection that was sure to follow. The phone rang. I answered. A voice on the other end whispered, "I am coming to you."

Midnight, Christmas Eve, five days after he arrived, Michael found my body, caressed and loved me and without a falter, slipped his penis into that formerly locked-down room and we made love. It was a miracle. But it was even more than that. For the act of intercourse, while an incredible expression of love, is still just intercourse. The miracle, the prayer that was answered resulted in an opening of my heart to the faith that our capacity to love is so large that all seeming impossibilities are a part of the leela, the maya, the illusion of life.

And now seven years later I still pray. And I write. And now I want to write a song. I want to write a song about God and shit and sex and finding love. I want to write a song about the lusciousness of life and all of its mysteries and of God and shit and of making love. I want to write a song about the body as a symbol of art and death and God and shit and juicy rock and roll sex that's still love. I want to write a song about thick masses of wet green moss and rivers and streams and amber adobe walls at dusk and making blissful love that takes me and my lover straight to God. I want to write a song about this body—naked and rearranged, strange, and volcanic—yet soft like the pure, virgin wool of a sweet baby lamb.

And I still want to write a song about God and shit and where simply peering through my tears into my lover's eyes will plunge me into the pure ecstasy of knowing God. I want to write a song about prayers that whisper incessantly and the cinnamon scent of wisteria in spring bloom and this body that's full of God and shit and my last breath that will be filled with knowing that this fucking life was all pure perfection. I want to write a song about this body that has been through the hell of the war of disease and is still the most beautiful cocoon where scars and colostomy bags are woven out of the finest silk. Where seemingly benign caterpillars are transformed into brilliant butterflies—defying the mysteries of nature that will always, I pray, continue to elude me; for the mystery of God is that gift that infuses me with the passion to continue to live this life. I want to write a song about that God, who yearns and sometimes screams within my heart to wake me up—begging me to know what it means to lose a colon, shit into a bag and still know undeniable and absolute love. I want to write a song. But what do I want most? What I want to do most is to sing.

Tanya Taylor and Pamela Thompson

I was fourteen years old. We came to the hospital to visit my grandfather, who was dying from a malignant brain tumor. I walked into the room to show off my new velvet skirt and first pair of high-heeled shoes. My always strong and brilliant Abuelo was doubled over in pain on a chair wailing in agony. I was shocked and terrified by the sight of him and I bolted out the door and ran down eight flights of stairs, twisting my ankle on the heels, not stopping until I hit the freezing air. A few days later I went into the hospital chapel and begged a God I was barely acquainted with to save his life. I had never known my father and was desperate to hold onto this man I loved so completely. He died a month later. His struggle with cancer and my family's subsequent grief was the defining event of my adolescence. I never felt as powerless as I did at that time.

I took my first acting class a month after his death. From the beginning I felt the wonder of being able to channel my personal expressions of pain into a role. Theater became my refuge and a way for me to process my own feelings. I went on to study acting professionally at Carnegie-Mellon University, Emerson College and H.B. Studios with the wonderfully eccentric Bill Hickey (nominated for an Oscar in *Prizzi's Honor*). While I was at Emerson, my acting teacher took our class to see the storyteller Spalding Gray at the Brattle Street Playhouse in Cambridge. I was nineteen years old. That night Spalding performed one of his lesser-known pieces entitled *Travels Through New England*. He sat behind a desk and told us a story about his life. He was honest and forthright. I will never forget his story of masturbating at Walden Pond so he could feel closer to Thoreau. It was a revelation. The seed of autobiographical monologue as a legitimate form of theater was planted in me that night, although it would take many years before I had the courage to stand onstage and open myself to that level of vulnerability in my work. However, once I did, there was no returning to conventional theater for me.

I left New York City for Santa Fe, New Mexico. I had never been to the Southwest before. I met Pamela in an acting class a month after I arrived. We had a brilliant teacher, Steve Johnson (who died of lung cancer at age forty-three in October 2001). He had the radical notion that theater could be used as a tool for self-realization and emotional healing. Our first assignment was to create an autobiographical monologue and perform it for the class. I began writing seriously for the first time and began creating original shows using the stories from my life as material.

In 1996 I created a one-woman show, *Honeymoon in India,* and went on to collaborate with Pamela on other shows. I got married and had a baby. Behind the scenes, our creative work was put on hold as Pamela's life became overwhelmed by her husband's fight with cancer and I ventured into the rocky but wonderful terrain of motherhood. Together we forged an alliance that has seen us through otherwise unbearable times.

Two years ago, my ex-husband called me from a business trip and ended our marriage. I was a stay-at-home mom with a two-and-a-half-year-old daughter, Chloe. All the plans I had for my life and our family became a moot point. I was starting over.

Suddenly at thirty-five years of age my life was being rerouted and I had no idea where I was going. I was starting over. I had never graduated from college, had no computer skills and desperately did not want to go back to waiting tables. I had not only myself to worry about, but a child to support. I was scared.

And so I prayed again, to a God I had come to know a bit better than when I was fourteen years old in that hospital chapel. I asked to be shown what I was supposed to do on this earth. I prayed for my true work to reveal itself. And I was a little bit pushy in that prayer. I wanted the answer yesterday. I did not have the luxury of time.

Then the idea came to me that Pamela and I should teach what we did best. The one thing I knew we both did well. So, we created The Life Monologue Project to support others in using the personal stories from their lives to create original and engaging theater. We taught them the process that we used to create our own shows.

One morning in the summer of 2000 I awoke from a very vivid dream. I saw the words THE CANCER MONOLOGUES floating over Lincoln Center in New York City. And I knew in an instant that I had been given an answer to my prayer. Pamela and I began to teach The Life Monologue Project to people in our community who had experienced cancer. The response to the first workshop/perform-ance was tremendous, both from the participants and from the audi-ence members who came to hear them tell their stories.

It is a privilege to be in the presence of people willing to share some of the most intimate aspects of their lives. Unlike watching an actor portraying a character with cancer, there is no possibility of distancing from our workshop participants when they themselves are standing onstage giving voice to their experiences of living with cancer. It is a profound first-hand sharing rarely experienced in our culture. In America, we have done everything possible to remove ourselves from the topics of illness and death. Our fear is often so great that we speak in euphemisms or turn away from really listen-ing to a friend or colleague who is going through such a deep expe-rience. We may isolate the people we love because of our own dis-comfort.

The Cancer Monologue Project is about shining a light on an aspect of life that is all too often either sensationalized by the media or denied. It is people stepping forth and sharing the experience of their lives with their community. Part of the experience is about having cancer. But it is never the complete story. For me, the greatest gift of working with these people is the realization time and time again that there is something much bigger than cancer in each story. That is their human spirit.

These monologues are created in a two-weekend workshop that culminates in a public performance at a theater. Ten participants arrive on a Friday evening for the first session. Pamela and I ask them to think about what they want to get out of this process. Most have never considered themselves writers and the vast majority have never even considered performing on a stage in front of an audience. Emotionally they usually range from somewhat nervous to utterly terrified. Much of the talk on that first evening centers on the fear of public speaking, and there is always one person who absolutely "knows" she will never be able to create a story for the performance. Yet something has pushed all of them to show up. Some kernel of hope, possibility, even excitement has gotten them to sign up for this workshop and set aside time in their already busy lives.

We ask them to put aside any preconceptions about what they can and cannot do. Each of them has walked into this room with everything they need to create a monologue. Pamela and I believe that each person has an incredible story within him or her. We simply give people the tools to let the story come out. We create a sacred and confidential space where it is safe to process and release any emotions that may arise. The space is nonjudgmental and we do not critique the pieces or make suggestions until well into the process. We ask people to just keep writing no matter what feelings arise. To put them on the page.

Pamela and I do not set ourselves apart as facilitators. We write and read and laugh and cry and share intimate aspects of our lives with the participants. We do not have cancer but we do have our humanity, and from that space we all have many stories to tell.

The second weekend of the workshop is devoted to helping shape and edit the raw material that has been written into cohesive pieces. Pamela and I support people in identifying emerging themes in their writing and ask them to think about what they most need to express at this point in their lives. Also, we assist them in creating transitions to make their pieces flow more smoothly and use vocal warmups and acting exercises to get them more comfortable and prepared for their one-night show. For the performance itself, our ten participants sit in a semicircle on a bare stage. There is a spotlight in the center. One at a time they stand and share their stories of living with cancer from the most personal and vulnerable place. One by one, ten people who sat in a circle in a small room two weeks ago are doing what they were certain they could never do. The audience is listening intently to every word. Each word, each breath, each tentative voice steps forward and grows in power and certainty with each line. The house lights come up. The audience is on its feet cheering, not letting the performers stop taking their bows for several minutes. A personal tragedy is transformed for one glorious moment into something greater, something beautiful. Each group we have worked with has been different. Each voice is holy. It is our greatest honor to be allowed to do this work. Every day I say thank you to my life and to this gracious Universe which has given me the job of collecting stories.

The vision for this work continues to evolve and grow. Pamela and I began this project with a deep commitment to offering these workshops free of charge to people who had cancer and their family members/partners. We will always be grateful to the City of Santa Fe Arts Commission, which gave us a grant that allowed us to offer the very first workshop. It became the prototype for all subsequent workshops.

It is our dream to teach workshops and do performances in communities all over the world. Pamela and I also hope to train facilitators to do what we do to take this meaningful work into their communities. As long as there is cancer, there are stories that exist behind the illness. We are interested in creating the space for all who have a story to tell to be able to stand on stage and tell it, each voice precious and unique. This project now has a life of its own and we will follow it wherever it leads.

Blessings,
Tanya Taylor

Theater has been one of the most important influences in my life. Not only did it provide an outlet for my abundant childhood energy (I'm sure, had I been born twenty years later, I would have been given copious quantities of Ritalin) but it offered an alternative community in which my creativity was nurtured and supported.

I've had some dynamic teachers in my life but it wasn't until I studied with Elaine Eldridge-Kern at the University of Wisconsin that I gained a deeper understanding of what theater can offer. Elaine is a talented actor and director with immense vision, passion and a deep commitment to her craft. Under Elaine's direction, we performed a weekly improvisational comedy show at the somewhat seedy and extremely smoky Club de Wash bar. Elaine treated the down-and-out bar's little stage like a church. There was no discussion about it: if we were going to work with her we had to agree to approach this space, the audience, and each other with reverence and respect. Initially it felt like trying to meditate next to a garbage heap. But I ended up learning that as long as I was one hundred percent committed inside, the audience would stay right with me. I also learned that if I could maintain the sanctity of the theater in this environment, I could do it anywhere.

After Madison I moved to Chicago and began a brief and bizarre stint in performance art. Standing in a gallery one Saturday evening, dressed in a corset and wig, spray painting a chicken, I realized that this world was a little too avant garde for a girl from Milwaukee. I left theater and performing altogether for many years, doing everything from AIDS research to advertising. It wasn't until I met with an insightful career counselor in downtown Chicago one chilly

September afternoon that I realized how much I missed the theater. After listening to me ramble on for more than an hour this wise man said, "When you spoke about your various jobs you told me what you did, when you spoke about theater you told me what you loved. You're extremely fortunate to know what it is you love to do, now you just have to find the faith and courage to do it." I felt stunned: this man had seen right through me. But I also felt challenged and I decided to give acting another try.

Soon after, I helped a friend move to Santa Fe. On the last day of my trip I took an acting class with a brilliant actor and coach, Steve Johnson. I knew right away that I had found my new teacher. Steve had us work with autobiographical material, which felt so much more immediate and intimate to me than working on scenes from plays. I decided to move to Santa Fe and began studying with Steve and that's where, in the summer of 1991, I met Tanya. Tanya strutted into the class on a hot Santa Fe summer afternoon dressed head-to-toe in black, with bleached blonde hair, heavy makeup and tons of attitude. I was instantly intimidated by her. She then got up in front of the class and proceeded to perform the most powerful and moving autobiographical monologue I had ever heard. I was so amazed by her performance that I overcame my fear and approached her. At first she didn't want to have anything to do with me, but I held on like a terrier. Finally she weakened, and we've been best friends ever since.

We both continued to do performance work in the very supportive community of Santa Fe and we both met and fell in love with our husbands here. It was Tanya who was there for me, when five months after my wedding day, my husband Sal was diagnosed with colon cancer.

For five years Sal and I traveled from hospital to hospital looking for hope and help, but there was very little conventional medicine could offer. So we explored alternative medicine—everything from teas, meditation, Tai Chi, ayurvedic medicine, to living at a raw foods institute where we ate only sprouts and juices while taking weekly trips to see a doctor in Tejuana. Sal even went to China to meet with Chi Gong masters who specialized in energy healing.

Before we got married we built a small house next to my mother-in-law Ana's house, as she was wheelchair-bound and it would be so much easier to assist with her care if we were living next door. Ana's health steadily declined and she was eventually diagnosed with Lou Gehrig's disease. For five years I took care of Sal, helped with Ana's care, and managed a jewelry store in downtown Santa Fe. Soon I began to feel the deep, undeniable burn-out that happens to so many long-term caregivers. I was depressed and had nightly anxiety attacks combined with sleepwalking episodes that left little energy for my busy days.

It was about this time that Tanya's marriage ended. She came to me one afternoon and said she thought we should teach writing and performance workshops together. As we had been writing and performing our own work for ten years it seemed to make sense, yet I was reluctant. I felt so depleted and I feared I wouldn't have much to give, but Tanya was extremely supportive as well as very hard to say "no" to. Saying "yes" to teaching the workshops was one of the best decisions I've ever made. Helping people find their voices and write their stories has given me more than anything I've ever done.

Shortly after we began offering these workshops to the general public here in Santa Fe, Tanya had a dream—literally—and called me to tell me that we needed to offer workshops to people with cancer. After dealing with the great expenses incurred from fighting cancer, I knew we needed to offer these workshops for free. We were fortunate enough to receive a grant from the City of Santa Fe Arts Commission to do just that. I also felt that given my own experience with cancer, I would be able to bring a deep understanding to working with these brave participants. What I didn't expect was that I would get so much back—from the intimate sharing of stories to watching the workshop participants on stage, taking their bows to standing-room-only audiences and beaming as if they've eaten uranium.

The Cancer Monologue workshops give participants something during a time in their lives when it seems that so much is being taken away. I am extremely grateful for all of the love and support that surrounded me and Sal during out battle with cancer, and now to be able to be there for people who are in a similar situation is profoundly enriching my life. It is a privilege to be a small part of each courageous journey.

My partnership with Tanya and our work with the Cancer Monologue workshops have turned what was one of the darkest periods in my life into something of value. I can't think of any better way to honor my own experience with cancer and the memory of Sal.

Pamela Thompson

ACKNOWLEDGMENTS

T anya and Pamela want to express their deepest thanks to the following people for their support and love: Wayne Carroll; Steve Johnson; Brian Garrido; Richard Becker; Dorie Hagler; Ira Gordon; Sascha Rice; Julia Hunkins; Adelma Roach; Joanna Bull, Joyce Bichler and Gilda's Club; Kim Bratt and Allyson Johnson; Tammy Walters; Shelley Morey; Monica Marchant; Deborah Rosenman; Elizabeth Martin; Catherine Owens, Annie Goodwin, Catherine Donavon and The Santa Fe Playhouse; Sabrina Pratt and the City of Santa Fe Arts Commission; Tony D'Agostino; Ron Andes; Krista Brooks; Lou Ann Asbury and St. Vincent Hospital Cancer Treatment Center; Laura Baynham-Fletcher and Place of Wellness at M.D. Anderson Cancer Center; Ursula Drabik; Steve and Becca Dixon and Flaming Dix Gourmet Foods; Peggy O'Mara; Jennifer Esperanza; Jonathan Lowe; Jim Terr; Donna Lee Goodbrod and Van Roy; Honey Harris; Hollis Walker; Wayne Sabato and The Santa Fe Performing Arts; Martha and Rob Shweder and The Playschool for the Arts; Christine Barber; KBAC-Radio Free Santa Fe; Andy Dudzik; Julia Goldberg and *The Santa Fe Reporter*; Robert Nott; Camille Flores; Dottie Indyke; Kristen Davenport and *The Santa Fe New Mexican*; Angela Krum at *Rosie*; *MAMM* magazine; *Natural Health* magazine; Carol Fass and Beth Scanlon of Carol Fass Publicity; Rosemary Zibart; Zelie Pollen, and the many local Santa Fe businesses for their generous support.

For the inspiration of their work we thank Spalding Gray, Natalie Goldberg, Julia Cameron, Alice Walker and Gangaji.

A special thanks to the amazing team at MacAdam/Cage who have put so much energy and heart into the making of this book: Anika Streitfeld, David Poindexter, Scott Allen, Pat Walsh, Amy Long,

Melanie Mitchell, Tasha Reynolds, Dorothy Carico Smith, Avril Sande and J.P. Moriarty.

With profound gratitude we want to thank all of the workshop participants and their families for their courage and willingness to share their stories and to our immensely supportive Santa Fe audiences.

With great love we want to thank Donna Loeb, Earl and Ellie Thompson, Lorraine Monnier, and our sweet angel, Chloe Grace.

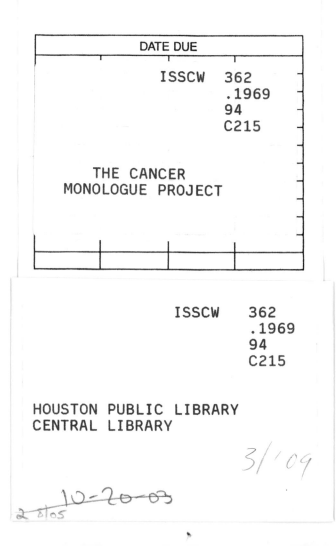